Pride  Aside

Steve Hutton

 Find us on
Facebook

www.PrideAside.org

Pride Aside Publishing Group
Madison, MS

Pride Aside Publishing Group (A division of Momentum Events, Inc.)
P.O. Box 2253
Madison, MS 39130

For privacy reasons, some of the names of individuals referred to in this book have been changed. Some of the individuals in this book are not actual individuals, but are composite individuals representing the actions or words of more than one person.

The quoted ideas expressed in this book (but not Scripture verses) are not, in all cases exact quotations, as some have been edited for clarity and brevity. In all cases, the author has attempted to maintain the speaker's original intent. In some cases, quoted material for this book was obtained from secondary sources, primarily print media. While every effort was made to ensure the accuracy of these sources, the accuracy cannot be guaranteed. For additions, deletions, corrections, or clarifications in future editions of this text, please write Pride Aside Publishing Group.

Scripture quotations are taken from:

The Holy Bible, New International Version (NIV) Copyright © 1973, 1978, 1984, by International Bible Society, Used by permission of Zondervan Publishing House. All rights reserved.

The New American Standard Bible® (NASB) Copyright © 1960, 1962, 1968, 1971, 1972, 1973, 1975, 1977, 1995, by The Lockman Foundation. Used by permission.

Holy Bible, New Living (NLT) Copyright © 1996. Used by permission of Tyndale House Publishers, Inc., Wheaton, Illinois 60189. All rights reserved.

The Message (MSG). This edition issued by contractual agreement with NavPress, a division of The Navigators, U.S.A. Originally published by NavPress in English as THE MESSAGE: The Bible in Contemporary Language copyright 2002-2003 by Eugene Patterson. All rights reserved.

The Holman Christian Standard Bible™ (HCSB) Copyright © 1999, 2000, 2001, by Holman Bible Publishers. Used by permission.

Cover Design by Dorian LaChance www.MagicByDorian.com
Page Layout by Service Printers, Inc., Flowood, MS 39232

ISBN: 978-0-9909283-0-0

For more information, please visit www.PrideAside.org.

Printed in The United States of America

This book is dedicated to my family, of which there are many.

To my parents, Ben and Sue Hutton, for providing a loving home and solid foundational guidance throughout my life.

To my wife, Joni, for being the calm in my life when I am stressed and for being my motivation when I am withdrawn.

To my youngest son, Michael, for being confident in who he is while the world tries to lure him to be someone else.

To my church family, Broadmoor Baptist Church, for being compassionate, supportive, and welcoming.

To my faith family around the country who have continued to pray and consistently check-in.

And to my oldest son, Ben, who learned for himself as well as taught others, that we all must put Pride Aside.

Contents

Foreword
By: Steve Farrar

I'm glad I read this book.

I think it could be of great benefit to you, or as a spouse and parent or grandparent who is seeking to lead your family on the narrow way of following the Lord Jesus Christ.

In fact, I see four benefits to this book.

It's a warning that the enemy is laying an ambush for your kids and grandkids.

Steve Hutton is gut-level honest on these pages about his love for his family and his desire to raise them in the truth of Christ. But Steve missed some warning signs that should have tipped him off that his son was in trouble. In all honesty, I missed some of the same warning signs with one of my sons. Steve will alert you to the warning signs and hopefully, you can begin to watch carefully for them in your own children.

It's an encouragement if you're exhausted from the battle.

If you have a son or daughter who is caught in the enemy's web and fighting against you and the Lord, Steve's transparent candor will help you. He pulls no Christian punches when it comes to the pain that his family has experienced. And, if you are in pain, you are going to recognize that other men who love Christ are fighting the same battle that you are. Elijah thought he was the only one who was fighting the battle and the Lord reminded him that he had seven thousand men who hadn't bowed the knee to Baal. Elijah wasn't alone and neither are you. Steve will help you to bear your burden as you read about his burden. It's strange how that occurs and the only explanation is in Galatians 6:2 (NASB): "Bear one another's burdens, and thereby fulfill the law of Christ."

It's realistic that this battle may not be over quickly.

If you're in family pain as Steve was and is, you obviously want the Lord to end the pain as quickly as possible. Yes, the Lord can fix anything in an instant because of His incomprehensible power, but sometimes He chooses to work in a human heart over a period of time. You and your family may be in the middle of that process. Obadiah Sedgwick once said, "that God may take time but He never wastes time." The Lord is all about timing. His goodness in timing is more precise than an atomic clock, and His precision in timing is never less than perfect. Romans 5:6 (NASB) declares that "at the right time, Christ died for the ungodly" and you can trust Him to do the work that only He can do in your family at the right time. He knows what He is doing—so don't put time expectations on the Lord. He has all wisdom and power and He knows better than you. Trust Him in that and know that He will give you new grace and mercy the first thing every morning as you wake up again to the battle.

It will spur you to pray for your children and grandchildren more consistently.

When I finished Steve's book that was my immediate take away.

I think it will be yours too.

Keep taking your kids before the Father and entrust them into His providential care. It's the safest place to be in the entire world. He loves your family more than you do. He's got your back. And you can trust Him with all of it. David said it best in Psalm 57:2-3 (NASB):

I will cry to God Most High;

To God who accomplishes all things for me.

He will send from heaven and save me.

Steve Farrar

Introduction

Pride  Aside

Thank you for taking time to read Pride Aside. I didn't set out to write a book. I only intended to spend time journaling on the computer to see if it would serve as therapy for me. Since I never took the time to talk to anyone about my feelings about our son's addiction, I expected it might be helpful to write down my thoughts. But after a few hours of writing, I noticed I had 5,000 words. Then after 15 days of writing, I noticed I had 65,000 words. Thus, a book was born completely by accident.

I want to warn you up front about one thing. You will notice at times I show signs of anger. This was real. I often found myself angry at circumstances and situations. At times I was angry with my son and sometimes I was angry with other people. I am not saying I had a right to be angry, but I was. So the words you read are authentic expressions of anger I was feeling.

I shared this with my good friend Steve Farrar, a best-selling author and speaker. In many ways Steve is my spiritual mentor. After listening he shared this Scripture with me:

> *Human anger does not produce the*
> *righteousness that God desires.* (JAMES 1:20, NIV)

The verse from James does not mean we should never get angry. It does mean, however, that we need to identify why we are angry and determine if it is just. Jesus was angered by many injustices. Jesus was angered by the moneychangers at the temple and by the self-righteous Pharisees, but He used anger to teach them truth. Looking back, I realize there were times when my anger was justified or righteous. But there were also times when it was not. For those times when

11

it was wrong, I have asked God's forgiveness and sought His power to live the righteousness God desires--according to His standards.

May I ask a favor of you? If for some reason you do not make it through the entire book, would you please read the last chapter? The first 21 chapters are filled with feelings of confusion, despair, self-doubt, and sometimes hopelessness. Chapter 22, however, helps tie all of those feelings together and offers clarity instead of confusion, joy instead of despair, assurance instead of self-doubt, and hope instead of hopelessness. Through this experience I discovered that the way to get to a place of clarity, joy, assurance, and hope in life is to put *Pride Aside*.

Chapter 1

Pride  Aside

*What sorrow for those who get up early in the
morning looking for a drink of alcohol and spend
long evenings drinking wine to make themselves
flaming drunk.* (ISAIAH 5:11, NLT)

The phone rang at 12:52 a.m. Some consider this late at night; others think it's early in the morning. Regardless, this was the type of phone call I had received numerous times before. Over the last five years these calls did not occur weekly, or even monthly, but they did occur several times. They usually occurred in waves or spurts. We might go a few months without a call like this, but when they started it was not unusual to receive several of these calls over the course of a few days or weeks.

"Mr. Steve, I am really sorry to have to call you, but it looks like we have a problem over here." Brian was calling. Brian was Ben's roommate. Brian and Ben had been co-workers off and on and very good friends for nearly a year. Brian is what we in Mississippi call a "good ole boy." He works hard. He is polite. He says, "Yes ma'am" and "No sir." He is clean cut and professional. (At least as professional as you would expect of a redneck from Pelahatchie, Mississippi.) Brian and Ben were both Sales Associates at a Ford dealership in Jackson. Sales Associate was what was printed on their business cards. But they were car men, car salesmen, and good ones. Brian has sold more cars than most of the other 35 sales associates at the dealership and is probably in line for management even though he is only 25 years old.

My son Ben is 23, and for the past five years has been a drug addict.

"Mr. Steve, I don't really know what has happened. Perry (the other roommate) and I were asleep and the next thing we know there is a girl here. Ben is yelling and screaming; we can't calm him down. She sprays him with pepper spray. The neighbors come out, someone called the cops, and there are cops everywhere."

I told Brian I would be right there. And while it wasn't a regular occurrence, once again I got dressed and left Joni, my wife of 27 years and Ben's loving mother, to go see what had happened this time.

At 1:02 a.m. I was in Bessie, my 13 year old GMC Yukon XL with 313,000 miles on it. I would love to have a newer vehicle. But I had to choose between a new car or replacing outdated things in our home because of the expense of dealing with Ben's addiction since it became apparent to us five years ago. I once heard Dave Ramsey, a syndicated radio host and leading financial counselor, say something like, "You know your car has been a good vehicle when you have had it long enough to name it." Dave spent an entire radio segment taking calls from people across America telling the world the name of their prized possession. Joni drives a 14-year-old Lexus RX300 with 202,000 miles. Her name, I mean its name, is Lexi. Joni hates that I have given her car a name as well, because it implies she will have to wait even longer before I can afford to buy her something nicer and newer.

Anyway, I was in my Yukon headed to Madison, a suburb of Jackson. Ben, Brian, and Perry were leasing one of my three bedroom rental properties in Madison. As I turned onto the highway out of our gated subdivision, I tried calling Ben's cell phone. Sometimes, when he was in a situation like this, I could keep him calm so things didn't get worse. For some reason he would listen to me. He trusted me. He loved me, and he knew I loved him, even though I despised his addiction. Since I knew the police were already involved, I assumed Ben would not answer his phone, but I wanted to try anyway. But there was no answer. So I called Brian for an update.

Brian said, "There are 10 or 11 cop cars here. I have never seen anything like it Mr. Steve, I just have never seen anything like it. He was fine when we went to bed, and then we woke up to this commotion and he was completely crazy. Fighting. We tried to calm him down but he just kept fighting."

I knew exactly what Brian was talking about.

Joni and I had seen this happen before. I had witnessed several crazy events like this much more often than Joni had. Fortunately most of them didn't occur in our home. Instead, I would go wherever Ben was and deal with the situation alone to shield Joni from seeing her firstborn in that state. Joni had seen Ben's rage on occasion, just not at the level I had.

Within five minutes I was turning onto Hunters Creek Circle. Ben's house, or my house really, was the second house on the right. There was very little room to park as the street was littered with marked and unmarked vehicles from the Madison Police Department.

Madison is a beautiful bedroom community five miles north of the Jackson city limits, separated only by the town of Ridgeland. When traveling north on Interstate 55 you don't fully realize when you have travelled from one town to the next. But the buildings begin to get nicer, the landscape around the highway signs begins to get prettier, and the affluence of the new surroundings becomes more and more apparent.

Madison is without question, at least in my opinion, the most beautiful and well-planned city in the state of Mississippi. Mary Hawkins Butler is in her 34th year as mayor, winning her first election in 1981 at age 26. She is one tough cookie as a leader, but her actions are purely out of the love for her city. She has held firm to her master plan over the course of her nine terms. This includes implementing strict housing covenants, which has allowed Madison to boast some of the priciest properties per square foot in the state. Then, as businesses clamored for the opportunity to service those households by bringing grocery stores, gas stations, clothing stores, restaurants, and other big box stores, she held even more firm as she made sure their appearance and structures met with the city's high standards. For instance, no orange can be found on the Home Depot. The golden arches of McDonald's are only three feet tall. The Burger King and the Texaco gas station are beautiful red brick buildings. A wall of transplanted trees behind the massive Wal-Mart Supercenter hides the semi-truck deliveries.

So I pulled up to the curb of 529 Hunters Creek Circle, one of the few rental houses I still owned in Madison. Mayor Mary does not like rental houses. Owner-occupied dwellings usually ensure better upkeep, better curb appeal, and better appraisals. However Mayor Mary and I had been friends a long time and she knew I followed all of the city's rules to a 'T' in maintaining my properties. But at this moment one of my properties was surrounded by her top-notch police force. They were dealing with an unruly tenant, who also happened to be my 23-year-old son.

As I walked down the driveway I was met by a girl I'll call "Gina." Gina looked rough. Joni and I first met Gina a year or so earlier when a friend of ours invited her to our Sunday School class. We had known of Gina prior to meeting her. She attended a private school that was a rival to the school Ben attended. I would not describe Gina as attractive, at least not anymore. At one time she was gorgeous--long jet-black hair, dark skin, and perfect curves. But her addiction had changed her features. Her face was pockmarked and covered with scabs. She was bleeding from the corner of her mouth, which made me wonder what had happened moments earlier. I had to remind myself that it was her addiction that made her look this way and inside she is still someone's beautiful daughter; but all I saw at that moment was her ugliness.

Gina started trying to explain, "I had to pepper spray him, Mr. Steve, I didn't want to but I had to. He hit me. He just kept coming. Perry tried to stop him, but he just kept coming. Perry would hit him and hit him, trying to make him stop, but he wouldn't settle down. He just kept coming at us."

I was beginning to see pieces of the picture.

It was like trying to put a jigsaw puzzle together. You look for puzzle pieces that have similar coloring or similar shading and you group those pieces together in order to get a general idea of what the full picture might look like. Once you have a general idea of where the pieces may best fit together, you can start concentrating on the details. It is at that point you start to notice the shapes of the individual pieces and try to actually fit some of those pieces together.

But I was not ready at that point for the details. I was still asking questions trying to get a general idea of the big picture. *Was Ben here? Was he inside the house or outside? Was he hurt? Was he alive? Was he under arrest? Would he lose his job? Would he lose the car he just bought with his own money for the first time ever? Would he need treatment again? Would he consider another treatment facility? Would he kill himself because he was tired of fighting and losing, again and again?*

I brushed past Gina and continued down the driveway to the carport at the rear of the house. I walked around Gina's new Lexus, which was in the driveway. How ironic, I thought as I walked around Gina's car. *My beautiful wife has to drive a 14-year-old version of this brand new automobile. My sweet wife has been a school teacher all of her adult life except for the time she took off when our sons were born to stay at home and nurture them until they started kindergarten. This same sweet wife gets up early, stays late at work, and even works weekends to be one of the best teachers in the county. But we cannot afford a new car for her because of what addiction has cost our family.*

And yet here is Gina.

She has been in and out of rehabs and treatment centers. She has had numerous jobs at strip clubs or restaurants where extra small shorts and tiny white t-shirts are the uniform of the day. Here she is driving around in a pretty new Lexus.

The entire scene was more than ironic. To me, at least in that moment, seeing her car was sickening, angering, and humiliating. I didn't know if my son was alive, dead, hurt, injured, or in custody. But all I could think about at the moment was how angry I was that Gina was leaning against her new RX400 and my wife had to drive a faded version.

Refocusing, I walked into the carport where I saw a gathering of people in the back yard. There was Ben, facing away from me, surrounded by five or six police officers. He was sitting on the ground, shirtless, his back covered in sweat, grass, and dirt. He was handcuffed with his hands behind his back. Some of the big parts of the puzzle were starting to be grouped together. I assumed he was headed to jail, again. *How many arrests was this? I've lost count.* And then there were the charges--usually there was more than one charge when he got arrested. *Was this five arrests and eight charges? Or did this make six arrests and nine charges?* I wondered how many charges would be added this time? Would he be facing his 10th? Or 12th? I also assumed he would not have a job the following day.

Wait. Let's mentally put the legal pieces of the jigsaw puzzle off to the left side of the card table. Let's keep those pieces separate from the job pieces, the living arrangement pieces, and car payment pieces. Let's put those mentally over on the right side of the card table. They were both parts of the big picture, but at that moment the coloring looked different, the shading was different, and the pieces needed to be separated before I started looking for details.

I had not even heard his voice yet, but I had been through this before. So all of these thoughts flooded my head once again. *He can't live in this house any longer. We had a deal: If you relapse, you move out. But his job is probably gone, so he can't move out, and he has no place to go. So again we will offer treatment. How many will this be? Five I think. What will he learn in number five that he didn't learn in number two or number four? Stop thinking about that now! Those are details. Focus. Get back to separating the pieces in general before you start looking for details.*

I was jolted back to the moment by a string of expletives: "(Bad Word) (Bad Word) (Really Bad Word) (Incredibly Bad Word)." Hearing Ben's first four words directed at one of the young Madison police officers at least let me know he was alive, breathing, and able to speak.

I personally knew some of the officers present.

About 20 years ago I was a Reserve Deputy Sheriff in Madison County. I still had several good friends on many of the area police forces. In the last 20 years my career consisted of managing a variety of events. I was Tournament Coordinator and Tournament Director of Mississippi's PGA TOUR event hosted at Annandale, a Jack Nicklaus signature golf course located in Madison. Recently I had been asked to develop an outdoor ice rink during the Christmas season, which surprisingly brought over 200,000 visitors to Madison in two years. Both events needed security, which kept me in close connection with many of my old friends in law enforcement.

Ben shouted again, "Take these cuffs off you (Bad Word) (Racial Slur), and I'll beat your (Really Bad Word) (Racial Slur) (Bad Word). You think you're bad? You (Really Bad Word) (Racial Slur), I will (Really Bad Word) (Bad Word) (Bad Word). Take these cuffs off of me."

Sgt. Steve Patrick, a patrol commander, was on shift that night and was standing with me. Since the bulk of his entire force was at my house, he decided to show up too. Steve is probably the nicest, most professional officer I have ever worked with. Steve and I spent hours planning security for Christmas On Ice, the outdoor rink I was managing. Steve is also African American, which made Ben's cussing tirades filled with racial slurs that much more embarrassing.

Mike Brown also walked into the carport that night. Mike was the first deputy I ever rode along with as a reserve deputy in Madison County. The first police call I ever responded to while riding with Mike was a "10-50 on Robinson Springs Road". Mike had to educate me that a 10-50 was an automobile accident. I knew nothing about being a law enforcement officer, and Mike taught me a great deal over the next few years. Now 20 years later Mike was not only a top officer with the Madison police department, he was also an elected constable for the county.

I could tell by the look on Mike's face when he walked in the carport that he had no idea why I was standing in the carport of 529 Hunters Creek Circle at nearly 2:00 a.m. that morning. "That's my boy," I said, nodding in the direction of Ben as Mike walked up. I could see the pain on his face as he said, "Aw man, Hutton. I knew you had a son who had some issues, but I had no idea."

Chapter 2

Pride  Aside

Since we respected our earthly fathers who
disciplined us, shouldn't we submit even more to
the discipline of the Father of our spirits, and live
forever? (HEBREWS 12:9, NLT)

"How do you spell Benjamin, anyway?" Joni and I were in the labor and delivery room at St. Francis Medical Center in Monroe, Louisiana, when she asked me that question. I guess the spelling of his name is something we should have researched more than an hour before we had to put a name on Ben's birth certificate. The sun had just risen on January 23, 1991, and we were watching the Today show between contractions. Operation Desert Shield had become Operation Desert Storm, and the first Gulf War was just completing its first week. The morning news was filled with Iraqi troops blowing up Kuwaiti oil fields. The name of the Israeli Deputy Minister of Foreign Affairs being interviewed by Bryant Gumbel scrolled across the screen: Benjamin Netanyahu.

Bam! That is how you spell Benjamin!

Many years before Ben was conceived, both Joni and I prayed for him. Joni and I met the first week of our first semester at the University of Southern Mississippi. We dated on and off while in school--on most of the time; off when we would have a big blow up argument. All of our friends laughed when we said we were engaged. We laughed somewhat, too. While such tumultuous dating habits lead to a disastrous marriage for many couples, Joni and I shared a secret weapon that would prove everyone wrong. We both shared a love for Jesus, and both shared a commitment to His Word and teachings, which included one man and one woman, married forever.

When Ben was born, I was a young PGA Professional, serving as Head Professional of Pine Hills Country Club just outside of West Monroe, Louisiana. We lived in Ruston, Louisiana, which we called Mayberry with a university. Through my golf connections we had 50-yard line tickets each year to watch the Bulldogs of Louisiana Tech and courtside seats for men's and women's basketball. The Lady Techsters were fixtures in the NCAA Final Four year after year and three time national champions. Life was good. We bought our first house and brought home our first child.

Joni had been a schoolteacher, but we decided to attempt to scrape by with her being a stay at home mom, at least for a few years. In 1992 we moved back to Madison, Mississippi, where Joni grew up and graduated high school. It is also the town we had moved to Louisiana from, just three years prior. Before moving to Louisiana, I served as the First Assistant PGA Professional at The Country Club of Jackson, and now we were moving back to the Jackson area where I would be Head Professional at Castlewoods Country Club, one of the nicest private courses in Mississippi at the time. Our household budget grew in size thanks to this new position, so we decided to grow our family as well. Along came Michael in 1994. We still talk about laying our eyes on Michael for the first time, and both gawking at the size of his big toe. Let me just say, the kid had an impressive big toe. I know they have charts to measure what percentile a baby is in based on the circumference of his head, weight, and length. If there was a chart to determine where he fell in comparison to other babies when it comes to the size of a big toe, I am certain Michael would have blown the curve.

We poured our lives into both of our boys. We also gave priority to our Southern Baptist church and our church family. We attended practically every Sunday morning and Sunday night. We loved Wednesday nights when about 400 of our fellow believers would have dinner together and then attend a prayer meeting, or a discipleship class, or choir practice. We even found ourselves there on some Tuesday nights when we would join up with a few friends and go to visit those who wanted to learn more about our church. As the boys grew older, they played church basketball, which took us back to the campus on Friday nights and Saturday mornings. I even did some part-time work organizing some of the recreation leagues for the church, and because I had a key, we were there even more.

Did I mention life was good?

We built a beautiful dream home at a neighboring country club, on Fairway Lane no less. The boys went to a Christian pre-school, and eventually were both enrolled in Madison County Public Schools. Madison schools are arguably the best in the state. The buildings are new and modern. The veteran teachers are empowered and energetic. The parents are involved and active. People in Jackson often enroll their children in private schools to assure their children a quality education. The Madison schools, however, are so good that many families sell their homes in Jackson and buy a more expensive home in Madison. They end up paying less overall because they don't have private school tuition factored into their budgets.

The boys both did well in school. Ben never had to study and easily made As and Bs. Michael struggled in math, which lowered his confidence in other subjects but he was able to get along just fine. With both boys in school, Joni returned to teaching at Madison Avenue Elementary, which is where both boys attended. This was great because she had weekends, summers, and holidays off with the boys.

By the time Ben was six and Michael was three, I left the world of being a country club professional to become the Tournament Coordinator and eventually Tournament Director for Mississippi's PGA TOUR event. My schedule was very flexible about 10 months out of the year. Only for the two months surrounding the tournament did I have to hunker down for extended hours. Over the next seven years my sons got to meet many famous golfers including John Daly, Hal Sutton, Bernard Langer, and Paul Azinger.

With my schedule being generally flexible, I was able to help coach some of the boys' teams. I knew nothing about soccer, so I limited my participation to a spectator on the soccer fields. But I knew about baseball, and I enjoyed coaching their baseball teams the most.

One year I had the privilege of coaching baseball with a great friend of mine, a man I truly admire. Andy Taggart and I coached the team our two sons were on, the Marlins. Andy is one of those guys who is fun to be around. His professional resume is unbelievable. He was a partner at one of the state's largest law firms, served as Chief of Staff for Governor Kirk Fordice, has co-authored two books on Mississippi politics, was elected and served as Madison County Supervisor, was CEO of the Mississippi Technology Alliance, and he served on boards of colleges and hospitals. I mean his resume is just ridiculous! Andy also has one of those "trophy wives," except Andy married his trophy wife the first time around. About 20 years earlier, Andy had married Karen, an elegantly beautiful woman. Together they had three boys, Rob, Drew, and Brad. Brad was on the

Marlins team along with Ben. The boys were 12 years old, and both were becoming very good at their sport. Brad especially had a breakout year and was being eyed by many other coaches who were looking down the road. The funny thing is, I don't know how Andy ever found time to work at any of the jobs I mentioned because he spent so much time with his family and his boys. The Taggart men were true outdoorsmen, with a particular bent toward duck hunting in the late fall. I learned a lot from Andy, especially in how he loved Brad, coached Brad, encouraged Brad, spoke to Brad, and all of the boys on the team for that matter.

It was the next baseball season, when Ben was 13, that I first sensed him slightly pulling away from me. I assumed it was his desire for independence. I began to see a young man trying to figure out who he was, yet not really sure who he wanted to be. Age 13 is when the boys who really don't like baseball typically stop playing. The teams are fewer, and coaches are usually the fathers of the exceptional players. I bowed out as a coach, but kept the books and statistics so I was still involved.

It was picture day at the baseball diamond on a brilliantly blue day in April of 2004. On picture day, players arrived at the ballpark an hour early and a photographer in a tent would take individual pictures of the boys. Then the photographer would sell parents an overpriced package consisting of an 8x10, two 5x7s, and 12 wallets. You could also buy a specialty product, like a banner for the 5x7 or a mug so you could sip your morning coffee while staring at your 13-year-old prodigy. After individual pictures, all of the players and coaches would line up for the team picture. The shorter players would take a knee (left knee down and right knee up) and the taller players would fill in the second row flanked by the coaches. On that day Coach Joe and his son Beck had their individual picture taken together. I thought, Wow, now that is cool. I had never seen a 13-year-old kid want to have his individual picture made with his dad. I wondered if maybe Ben would like to do that with me.

I walked over to Ben and put my arm around him and mentioned how cool Coach Joe and Beck's picture was. Then I asked if he might want us to have a picture made together. All of us have those moments that are etched into our psyches like a branding iron burns a permanent mark into flesh. That became one of those moments for me. Ben swirled out from under my arm and gave me a stare of disgust like I had never seen before. Then he told me to go stand elsewhere.

I remember tears welling up in my eyes because I had never felt that type of disapproval from him. He had no idea that my feelings were shattered. I backed away from everyone and hid the fact that I was about to cry. I was not only shattered; I was scared. That simple act was my first clue that fathering was about to change.

Until now, my words of instruction were taken as absolute truth, simply because I was Dad. But that simple gesture let me know that he was forming his own opinions, coming to his own conclusions, and would soon be charting his own path in life. I would have to father from a different perspective from that day forward. My arguments would have to be crafted more from a point of reason than simply from the stance of "It is so, because I am your dad." It wasn't that I could no longer punish or discipline Ben at age 13. However, I knew I would need to be very intentional to provide reasoning behind the punishment if it were to be truly effective.

Looking back on that picture day April 2004 has caused me to wonder a lot. If I could have looked 10 years in the future to April 2014 and zeroed in on the backyard of 529 Hunters Creek Circle and known what was to come, I wonder if I would have done things differently? I wonder if I should have guided Ben to focus less on sports and focus more on determining who he was in Christ? I wonder if I would have taught him more about prayer and less about leaning on his own abilities? I wonder if I could have helped him develop a healthy, respectful fear of his earthly father, so that one day he would have that same healthy, respectful fear of his Heavenly Father?

I wonder, I wonder, I wonder.

I wonder what role I played in the sequence of events that led to his 6th arrest that night in Madison, being charged with his 11th and 12th crimes. As parents we all wonder. And most of us would like to peek into that crystal ball to see where our kids would be and possibly change our parenting accordingly. But we cannot. We can't see into the future. We can only trust that God knew what He was doing when He placed that child in our care, and trust that He gives us the tools and strength to endure the decisions the child ultimately makes on his or her own.

Still, I wonder.

Chapter 3

Pride  Aside

Where there is no guidance, the people fall,
but in abundance of counselors there is victory.
(PROVERBS 11:14, NASB)

As fun as baseball was, Ben found he excelled on the football field because of his speed. Near the end of his seventh grade year at Madison Middle School, the PE classes turned their attention to spring football. Ben had played some YMCA football and some recreational football, where all of the coaches doted on his speed. But seriously, what can you tell about a fifth or sixth grader? The biggest kid at that age may be medium sized in the twelfth grade. The fastest kid at that age may struggle to keep up in a few short years. The accolades of the earlier years were nice, but we paid them no attention.

At the end of seventh grade spring practices, the coaches took all of the boys and dressed out four teams: red team, blue team, green team, and gold team, as I recall. Then all of the parents were invited to something of a round-robin competition, where each team would have playing time against each of the other teams. This was different than recreational football. This was 100 or more boys, and as much as Michael's big toe would have ranked him in a high percentile, big brother Ben's overall stature would have ranked him near the bottom. Ben was shorter than most, definitely skinnier than most; but to our amazement, he truly was faster than them all.

He played a defensive back position. Regardless of which side of the field a running back would break loose, Ben would catch him before he got to the end zone. It didn't matter where the runner went; Ben would catch him. At one point Brad Taggart's parents, Andy and Karen, turned to us and laughed and said something like, "He seems to make it his mission not to let anyone get past him."

So we took notice that day. Ben was fast. And he loved football. Suddenly football was all Ben talked about. Still, eighth grade football in Madison had over 100 boys involved. Fast or not, it would be easy to get lost in the crowd of 99 other boys.

During the summer I saw David Thames, not only a good friend but also my insurance agent and the guy I share a deer camp with. David told me that he and his wife Susan were transferring their soon-to-be ninth grade son to Madison-Ridgeland Academy, a local medium-sized Christian school, very well known for their athletic programs.

Soon, Joni and I visited the school and we were impressed with their Christian focus on education. The faculty was just as free to use the Bible in the classroom as they were a textbook. The weight room also looked like it should have been in a college rather than a high school. The staff really took an interest in Ben and made him feel like they really wanted him to become a student there. Looking back, I assume they make every student and parent who is willing to shell out $6,000 per year feel like they would love to have the student attend there. But that's to be understood. So we signed on the dotted line and enrolled Ben in school at MRA.

The first football game Ben played in that fall was against Leake Academy. I have always been a photography buff, so I offered to take pictures from the sidelines. I was surprised to see Ben take the field on offense. I had not attended any of the practices, so I had no idea what position he was going to play. This whole football parent thing was new to both Joni and me. I didn't realize there were unwritten rules in the South about being a middle school or high school football parent. You see, parents are supposed to go watch their boys practice after school; they are supposed to buy ads in the program and put their son's picture in the ad; they are supposed to talk to other parents constantly about what teams we are going to play and who we have to beat to make the playoffs. I'm kidding about the unwritten rules, of course--parents aren't *supposed* to do any of that. But those are the things they all did. And before long, Joni and I did them as well.

So in that first game of the season, I was surprised when Ben took a handoff. He went around the left side and began running down the near sideline, in perfect view of my new Canon Rebel. Next thing we knew, boom--touchdown!

Really? I didn't know he played offense! He is so little.

I found it hard to believe they would even give him the ball, but they did. And he scored! Did I get any pictures of that? Yes, I did! And they look pretty good actually.

So maybe there is something to this football thing.

The eighth grade football season came and went. Then a few months later came spring. I didn't realize what a big emphasis football coaches placed on the spring track season for their football players. All players were expected to participate. This kept them in good shape throughout the spring, and speed drills for the sprinters helped on the football field as well. Ben was obviously tapped as a sprinter, which he loved. He despised running long distances. He primarily ran the 100-meter, 200-meter, 4x100 relay, and 4x200 relay. Occasionally he was asked to do another event depending on how the team stood in their meet, but these were his main events.

Just like football, Ben excelled in track. He won pretty much every race he participated in, though he was usually going up against ninth graders as well.

Summer arrived, but that no longer meant the usual student's summer vacation. All athletes were required to participate in summer workouts and weight training. At the end of the school year, a summer weight training schedule was distributed. It involved workouts about three days a week for about six weeks until the first part of July. After that, a short break was given. But football camp started near the end of July as teams started getting ready for the first Friday night lights of August. But in Ben's case, it was Thursday night lights since he was just entering the ninth grade.

This new lifestyle of middle school and high school athletics meant new fathering challenges. Several things were about to occur that would test the way I had planned to parent. Soon there would be a desire for a driver's license. Which means there would also be a desire to get a car, or for most Mississippi boys, a jacked-up pickup truck. Accompanying a license and a truck would be extraordinarily high insurance premiums. Probably just like most of you, I had read books on parenting, I had attended a few parenting seminars at church, and every year I had heard a few sermons dedicated to strong parenting. So I had developed ideas about how to best handle this stage of life.

I mentioned earlier a radio host named Dave Ramsey. He was on the air for about three hours in the afternoons and I often listened to him if I was driving during his show time. Dave often talked about creating a "501-Dave Plan" for his children. The children would be expected to earn their cash through a part time job or through doing chores around the house. Whatever the kids saved, the 501-Dave Plan meant that Dave would match those funds specifically for the purpose of buying a car-- but only a modest car would be considered, and the car had to be paid for in cash.

I had always liked this idea and planned to implement it. I believed that building a strong work ethic during the early impressionable years would surely pay dividends into adulthood.

But now I began to wonder, *How does this happen for a high school athlete? He doesn't have time to work in the fall and afterward his spare time is consumed in the weight room, off season track meets and practice, and extensive summer workouts.*

So I talked with other parents.

Keep in mind these were primarily the parents who could afford an extra $6,000 per year for private school tuition. And from them I began to hear a different point of view. They were saying that if a young athlete is working hard in school, keeping good grades, going to practice after school all year long, doing summer workouts, and sweating through two-a-days in the pre-season, then that is considered his job.

Their mindset was that it was OK for Daddy to buy the car and for Daddy to pay for insurance as long as the young athlete was "working" hard, academically and athletically.

Interesting. High school athletic training as work.

I had never considered that before. But soon I would give in to this mindset--which would be the first of many compromises I would make in raising my two sons.

Chapter 4

Pride  Aside

For if someone does not know how to manage his
own household, how will he care for God's church?
(1 TIMOTHY 3:5, NASB)

In 2005 a teen in Mississippi was allowed to obtain a driving Learner's
Permit on their 15th birthday. Six months later they were allowed to
get an Intermediate License, which gave them permission to drive
unaccompanied during the day but not after a certain time at night. Then
at 16 that same teen could attain a full-blown driver's license.

Ben's birthday is January 23, less than one month after Christmas. If
Ben was going to have a used vehicle to drive, and if Daddy was going to
pay the tab for said vehicle, it made sense to me to combine a Christmas
and birthday present. This way I would not spend several hundred dollars
on frivolous gifts at Christmas only to give him a truck on his birthday.
Instead, I would give him a truck at Christmas and tell him the truck
was a combined gift and maybe we could look at some accessories for his
birthday. It sounded logical and reasonable to me!

Thus I bought Ben a truck for Christmas 2005 when he was age 14 years,
11 months.

As I just typed that sentence, I admit I had to stop for a moment, lean back in my chair, cross my arms, and read it back to myself a few times. Looking back I see so many areas of compromise that baffle me to this day. You may have just read that sentence and verbally condemned me; possibly even labeled me a complete idiot. And you know what? I agree with you. At least I do now. The power of hindsight is exponentially greater than the power of on-the-fly decision-making. Maybe that is why I felt so compelled to put pen to paper, so to speak, and record the sequence of events that ultimately brought me into the back yard full of police officers at 529 Hunters Creek Circle several years later.

Did buying Ben a truck cause him to spiral out of control years later? Of course not. Were there 75 other boys and girls in Ben's grade who also received a vehicle that year? Yes there were. Did they all spiral out of control as a result? Of course not. Were there more than 500 kids in our city who received such a gift at that age? Were there several thousand kids who received such a gift that year across our state? Were there hundreds of thousands who received such a gift that year across our country? Of course. Did they all spiral out of control in the years to come? Of course not. But can I look back and identify benchmark moments in time, coupled with dozens of other compromising parenting decisions that in my mind contributed to his years of struggling? Yes I can, and this would be one of those benchmarks.

The truck was not even very nice. It was six or seven years old and had over 100,000 miles on it. But it did have several modifications that made it appealing to any teenage Mississippi boy. It had a lift kit, which means it was "jacked-up" eight inches higher than it came from the factory. It had oversized mud tires, a staple in our little yuppie town. And man was that truck loud! Aftermarket pipes and mufflers let everyone know this truck was coming long before their eyes could witness its arrival. We called Ben's truck "The Mudder."

But enough about the truck. It's not the point. The point is I never gave Ben an opportunity to learn the value of taking ownership of such a possession. I robbed him of the lessons that could have been learned in working part-time on the weekends to participate in the purchase. I stole from him the pride of taking some of his own earnings and applying them toward the purchase, or toward the cost of insurance, fuel, or maintenance. I could have implemented a 501-Steve Plan and matched his earnings two for one, or three for one. Then at least he could have participated at some level in the purchase.

But instead I did it all for him.

Over the next several years I would do dozens of things for him. And while no single act was bad in and of itself, the sum total of all of these acts would ultimately contribute, at least in my opinion, to producing a young man who had no concept of delayed gratification. I have heard some experts refer to this as "affluenza," a cross between "affluence" and "influenza." This is the constant desire to have what I want, when I want it. It's a condition resulting from life being too easy.

So let's break this down.

Was Ben brought up in a loving home? Was he taught the difference between right and wrong? Was he allowed and encouraged to develop, maintain, and pursue a personal relationship with a Holy God and a forgiving Savior? Did his parents model for him what it looked like to work hard, maintain a clean house and a pretty yard, give generously to those less fortunate, and obey the laws of society? Yes, yes, yes, and yes. But did his parents actually help him implement these lessons into his own life, or did they simply model it?

When I wrestle with this question I think of two stories recorded in the Bible. A disciple named Matthew wrote about two interesting experiences involving Jesus and His twelve disciples. Even if you aren't familiar with many Bible stories, you may have heard of these events. Jesus had been preaching to a large crowd and had also healed many sick people. Near the end of the day the disciples knew everyone was hungry. They suggested Jesus dismiss the crowd so the people could leave the remote area and go elsewhere to find food. But Jesus said to the disciples, "They do not need to go away. You give them something to eat" (Matthew 14:16, NIV). The disciples came up with five small loaves of bread and two small fish. So Jesus directed the crowd to sit down and He took the fish and bread, looked to heaven and gave thanks, then broke the food into pieces to be distributed to the people.

This is where the story becomes interesting. Think about what Jesus did. In the midst of a crowd of people stood the God of universe in human form. He could have snapped His fingers and made food appear in everyone's lap. He could have filled the crowd's bellies to satisfaction without anyone eating a single bite. But instead, Matthew 14:19 notes that Jesus gave the fish and loaves to His disciples, then the disciples gave the food to the people. Jesus not only modeled for His disciples, He also allowed them to experience the miracle by doing the work themselves.

After everyone ate and was full, there were 12 baskets full of leftovers! The Bible states there were 5,000 men, not counting women and children. So it's possible there were 10,000-15,000 people who were fed that day.

Right after that event, Jesus told His disciples to get into a boat and go ahead of Him to the other side of the lake while He dismissed the crowd. Late into the night (a few hours before sunrise) their boat was still a considerable distance from land and was being bombarded by waves and wind. Right then Jesus went to the disciples, walking on the water! As

He approached the boat the disciples thought He was a ghost. Jesus told them not to be afraid, and assured them it was indeed Him. Peter, one of the disciples, wanted proof. He asked Jesus to allow him to walk on the water. Jesus invited him, so Peter got out of the boat and walked toward Jesus. But because of the wind and storm Peter got scared and then began to sink. Though he had briefly done the impossible, Peter's fear and doubt caused him to fail.

This story reminds me that it is OK to let our children fail. Jesus could have allowed Peter to successfully walk on water during the storm for the rest of the night. Or Jesus could have calmed the storm, let the sun shine, and made it easier for Peter. But Jesus didn't do that. Instead, He allowed Peter to experience fear. He allowed Peter to experience doubt. He allowed Peter to experience failure. Jesus didn't set up Peter to fail, but He allowed it.

So let's go back to my earlier questions. Did I, or we, model positive things into our sons' lives? We did. But did we often find ourselves doing their work for them? And did we help with the science project more than we should? Or did we even do the whole science project for them sometimes? Ultimately, did we make life so easy for them that we robbed our children of many life lessons?

Steve Farrar is considered one of the most innovative and effective Christian communicators in the country. He is the author of the best selling book *Point Man – How A Man Can Lead His Family*, as well as a dozen or more other books I've read including *Finishing Strong, King Me, Battle Ready, True Courage,* and *God Built*. I have hosted Steve in more than 20 men's conferences and heard him speak truth in over 100 sessions to men. Once I heard him tell about a young mom who was scared to let her son play football. She told Steve she was scared he was going to get hurt. Steve jokingly said she should not worry if her son would get hurt, because he was definitely going to get hurt! That is why they call it football. You buy the kid pads, you help him train, and you allow him to get hurt.

And getting hurt is OK.

There are so many life lessons that come from this one simple story. And the funny thing is, I knew those lessons. I even modeled them. But with perfect hindsight, I can see so clearly where I robbed my boys of the opportunity to "get hurt." I didn't allow them to fail and learn from that failure on their own.

Chapter 5

Pride  Aside

Have nothing to do with the fruitless deeds of
darkness, but rather expose them.
(Ephesians 5:11, NIV)

Ninth and tenth grades were both pretty good years for Ben as far as we could tell. Social media was in its infancy. Texting was just becoming the norm, and Facebook, Instagram, and Twitter had not yet become universal. There was one incident where some of the neighborhood boys did the camping in the woods thing. Joni had a feeling I should go check on them at 2:00 a.m., so I did. I found the boys had some alcohol, which was warning sign #2.

Ben's best friend around that time was Jeremy. Jeremy was hilarious and quite unfiltered for a kid that age. He was also afflicted with "affluenza." His parents were nice folks, but they lived more of a rock star lifestyle than any other kid's parents I had ever met. Jeremy always had a new truck, would tear it up, and would then be rewarded with another. He always had the latest in anything he wanted. We did intercept a couple of odd text messages between Ben and Jeremy about some cold medicine pills, which Ben explained away. But looking back that was warning sign #3.

Tenth grade was coming to a close. As a sophomore, Ben got a great deal of playing time on the football field behind some of the state's best graduating athletes. He was the starting kick-off return specialist, and was able to rotate in every game at running back to give the starting senior running back a rest. The MRA Patriots made it to the playoffs but ended their season losing the state championship game. Losing the state championship I think was a benchmark moment for Ben in a unique way. He was a little disappointed not to get a championship ring, but not devastated by any means. He was a sophomore. He would be able to return the next year and the year after that, most assuredly as the starting tailback both years. But in that locker room after the state championship loss to Jackson Prep, Ben saw those seniors that he had been awe struck by the last couple of years sobbing on each other's shoulders. These were 17-year-old giants of men (at least in Ben's eyes) crying; and I mean like snot coming out of your nose kind of crying! At that moment he resolved to work harder than ever before--lifting, running, training--and made it his mission not to be crying after the last game of his senior year.

It was Friday afternoon late in the spring of 2007, Ben's sophomore year in high school. Track season was winding down and there was a regional meet out of town the following day. It would determine who would qualify for the state track meet. The coaches had entered Ben in several events going up against seniors, and they felt sure he would qualify for the state track meet in at least one or two events.

Ben called me after school just to check in. "Hey Dad, about to leave school with Craig and Melanie and just go hang out, then we have that big party tonight at the Country Club." "Sounds good," I replied, "Who's Craig?" Ben responded, "I'm not sure if you know him; he's in my grade. I just really got to know him. His mom is a doc."

Don't you love it when your children make new friends?

It often says a great deal about their character. It says they are open, inviting, or just downright friendly. Sometimes you even see it as a reflection of yourself. People like my children! I have done well as a parent. Others are drawn to them. How wonderful it is they have made a new friend.

Over the next few years, however, gaining a new friend was often a red flag that needed to be explored. I did not realize it in the spring of 2007, but eventually I would see a pattern emerge when Ben suddenly had a new friend.

Many kids seem to migrate to other kids who are like them. Athletes and cheerleaders often hang out with athletes and cheerleaders. Smart kids hang out with smart kids. Children with learning issues often hang out with children with learning issues. We never encouraged our children to be a part of a clique; instead we encouraged them to befriend everyone and see others as Jesus sees them. Still, children often befriend those most like themselves.

What I would learn over the next few years is that addicts always hang out with addicts. They don't want to use alone. If someone else is using alongside them, it makes them feel better about their own use. The problem, at least in our little haven in suburbia, is that it's not so easy to spot the addicts, or perhaps at this stage of Ben's story I should say the abusers.

The first thing we should agree on is that in the eighth, ninth, and tenth grades, there are very few addicts. There are several teens, however, who are beginning to abuse alcohol and drugs to some degree. A few of these unsuspecting young men and women are on a path to becoming addicts. But at that point in middle or high school, most are simply experimenting and occasionally abusing.

Disclaimer!

I make no claim to have any in-depth medical knowledge, psychological knowledge, or pharmacological knowledge. I am simply a parent who has walked through a very interesting journey over the past several years and has formed several opinions. I believe these are educated opinions in the sense that I have read many books, sat through several family educational programs at various drug rehab facilities, and have researched many studies and papers written by men and women far more educated than me. So I base much of what I am about to say on my own personal opinion, which at least in my mind, is "somewhat" of an educated opinion.

Here are two main distinctions you should know.

First, substance abuse is not the same as substance addiction. According to teenshealth.org, the difference between the two is very slight; but there is a difference. Substance abuse means using an illegal substance or using a legal substance in the wrong way. Addiction begins as abuse, but abuse doesn't come from addiction. A person can abuse alcohol or drugs without having an addiction. For instance, just because "Sara" smoked pot a few times or "Jason" took a friend's pills at a party does not mean either has an addiction. It does mean, however, that both of them abused a substance, which could lead to addiction.

Second, addiction means a person has no control over whether he or she drinks or uses a drug. Someone who's addicted to cocaine has grown so used to the drug that he or she has to have it. Addiction can be physical, psychological, or both.

Physical addiction means a person's body actually becomes dependent on a substance, which could be anything from nicotine to heroin. It also means a person has developed a tolerance to that substance, so he or she needs a larger dose than before to get the same effect. Someone who has a physical addiction may experience physical withdrawals when they stop using a particular substance.

Psychological addiction may cause a person to feel overcome by the desire to have a drug. They may lie or steal to get it. Most addicts experience a combination of physical and psychological addiction. A person crosses the line between abuse and addiction when he or she is no longer trying the drug to have fun or get high, but has come to depend on it. This person's whole life centers on the need for the drug and feels there is no choice whether to take it. We will get more into this later.

About 10 minutes after Ben and I hung up he called me back, "Hey pops, everyone is OK, but I bumped into a guy at a stoplight and dented his tailgate. He's not mad or anything, he just wants to know if we want to turn it in on insurance or not." I spoke to the man over the phone and he indeed was very nice. Ben's big ole' jacked-up Chevy Silverado sat a good bit higher than this man's pretty new Ford F-150, and Ben apparently let his foot off the brake at a stoplight and creased the man's tailgate.

I told him I would be right there.

I arrived at the parking lot of the Chevron station where they had pulled their two vehicles, just a few blocks south of Ben's school. Ben was more talkative than usual, especially since he just put a $600 crease in the back of someone else's brand new F-150. Melanie was smiling, but it seemed her eyes were searching my expressions and demeanor to determine if I was angry or not. I got to meet Ben's new friend Craig, a nice young man who looked me in the eye and gave me a firm handshake. Good first impression. We made arrangements for the F-150 driver to go get an estimate, and I would pay him cash so our pricey insurance premiums would not become even pricier. He went out of his way to comfort me as a dad, pointing out that my son was not goofing around, was very polite to him after the incident, and this was just a careless mistake.

Have you ever had a weird feeling? But not weird enough to really pursue why you had the feeling in the first place? If you were in the presence of someone who had just had a minor fender bender and witnessed him or her trip or stumble, then that might give you a weird feeling to the point of investigation. You might wonder, *Had they been drinking?* You might smell their breath or look inside the vehicle. But the weird feeling I had was not that strong; it was just there. After all, the kids had just left school 90 seconds before and had driven maybe 10 blocks! But I remember driving off and thinking, *That was odd. Ben was a tad more smiley than usual. Melanie sure was trying to gauge my temperature of the whole situation. Craig was nice, but I don't really know him well enough to know if that firm handshake is normal or not.* There was nothing there I could pinpoint; just the thought of *that was odd.*

Looking back I realized my weird feeling was on target.

Ben's new friend Craig, as you may recall, is the son of a physician. Craig had helped himself to some of his mom's prescription medication that morning before heading to school. Ben and Craig had taken some of the pills during the day at school. Little did I know at that time, but they were about to take several more pills before the night was over.

I next spoke to Ben a couple of hours later, right before several kids were going to a combination end of the year and birthday party for a young lady in Ben's class. Ben's words were garbled over the phone. I pressed him for more information about where he was and whom he was with as I tried to determine if I should go find him or not. He said a few things that made no sense, then he said he would call me right back. Then he hung up. I tried to call him back but his phone was off--going straight to voicemail.

Joni and I talked about what we needed to do and tried to determine a quick plan of action. But we did not have a clue what we needed to do specifically. This was not covered anywhere in the best seller *What To Expect When You're Expecting*. We knew we needed to find Ben. We knew we needed to make sure he was safe and others were not in danger. And we agreed about one thing that was very important; we knew we needed to alert other parents of the children with Ben so if their child was in danger, there might be a chance to head off a catastrophe. This was the hard one. We needed to alert other parents that our son was under the influence of something, and that they might need to check on their own child. Seriously? Can you imagine the embarrassment we were about to put ourselves through? The parents of the cool kid who had good grades, excelled in athletics, and was in church every time the door was open were about to call other parents and tell them their kids may be drunk or high? We did not want to do that. We did not want to humiliate ourselves that way. But we knew we had to make the calls.

We would want other parents to do the same for us.

Finally I was able to get Todd on the phone. Todd was a friend of Ben's who was at the same party. Todd told me something wasn't right with Ben. Todd then gave Ben the phone, and this was where I made one of the worst mistakes I have ever made.

Two things I need to say about the mistake I am about to describe. First, it turned out OK, but it was still a mistake. Second, I absolutely did not know what I was doing; I was reacting out of anger and was not clear-headed. When Todd handed him the phone, I said these words to Ben, "Get in your truck right now and get home. If you are not home in 10 minutes I am coming down there and getting you in front of everybody!" Click. We hung up. Then it occurred to me what I had just done. I just told my teenage son, who has possessed a driver's license for less than six months, who was either intoxicated or high, to get in a three-ton, jacked-up weapon of steel and drive as fast as he could to our house. The second I realized what I had done I called Todd back but Ben had already left.

I asked Todd to put the father of the girl hosting the party on the phone. I introduced myself, apologized for bothering him, and made him aware of what was going on with Ben. I told him I felt like whatever Ben had done had occurred prior to him arriving at the party, and in no way was I suggesting his daughter's birthday party was to blame. But I wanted him to know what had happened so he could check on any of the other students who might have arrived with Ben. He was grateful for the heads up.

Because of the pipes and exhaust on Ben's Chevy, we could hear him long before we could see him. Joni and I were waiting in the driveway for Ben to arrive. Soon it was obvious he was driving very fast. He whirled into the driveway and defiantly slid out of his truck, angry that we would dare instruct him to come home. At least that's what we could make out of the gibberish coming from his mouth. He eventually calmed down enough to come into the house and sit on the couch, but not before trying to ride a skateboard in the driveway. For some reason he felt like hopping on his brother's skateboard for a few minutes before coming inside. We saw that the right front fender of his truck was smashed and soon discovered Ben had hit a brick column protecting pumps at the gas station. I later went to see if there was any damage at the gas station, but there was not.

Inside the house, Joni and I got very little information. We asked Ben if he had been drinking, and he said no. We asked if he had taken some type of drugs, and he said yes. We asked what, and he said he did not know. We asked what color or what shape it was, and he said it was a big white thing. We all sat in silence for a short time, and finally Ben leaned his head back on the couch and went to sleep.

I called Craig's mom. Again, we wanted to be the parents who did the right thing. Even though we were embarrassed, we needed to expose the darkness. It took Craig's mom a few hours to get any useful information out of her son. Craig had supposedly taken just one pill and was not high; he just was not quick to give his mother information. Ben had taken many pills, which we later discovered to be Klonipin.

To this day, we still do not know exactly how many he took.

Klonopin is benzodiazepine, much like Xanax. Klonipin and Xanax are both typically used as a treatment for panic disorder. In today's world, these are very common to find in bathroom medicine cabinets all across America. Craig had taken the bottle, which probably had 12-15 pills in it to school that day, at the request of Ben. Craig took a pill, a couple of other kids took a pill, but Ben had several. He took one early during the school day, and one later in the school day. He took another after school. And at some point later that afternoon he grabbed several and took them all at once.

Ben had not simply gone to sleep on our couch. He had passed out. This was his first semi-overdose, and we did not even know it. By the time we had the information we needed, several hours had passed and what was done was done. We stayed awake and watched him the rest of the night just to make sure he was breathing.

The next day was the regional track meet. I woke Ben up early and told him to get dressed. He was still somewhat high, and moved more like a zombie than a sprinter. We thought making him run in the Mississippi heat might be a good punishment. And it was. He threw up numerous times, and finished nearly last in every race he was supposed to win.

The following day he and I sat down and had a somber conversation about what all had happened. We came up with a reasonable punishment of being grounded and things like that. Ultimately I felt like he was more shocked about what he did than Joni and I were. What he had done scared him.

He was truly sorry.

Chapter 6

Pride  Aside

*Everyone who competes in the games goes into
strict training. They do it to get a crown that will
not last; but we do it to get a crown that will last
forever.* (1 CORINTHIANS 9:25, NIV)

Ben's junior and senior years came and went faster than any parent would
ever wish. In his junior year of football, Ben started at tailback and had
a beefy fullback in front of him named Brandon Self. It was not long
before the two had the nicknames of Thunder and Lightning. Brandon
(Thunder) would pound it off guard and off tackle, time after time after
time. And just when the opposing team's defenses were worn down, Ben
(Lightning) would strike and turn the corner and be gone. Ben had good
stats his junior year, his grades were good, and track season produced
more blue ribbons than Aunt Bee's pies at the Mayberry County Fair. I
even upgraded my camera from the Canon Rebel to a Canon 20D his
junior year. For his senior year I upgraded again to a Canon Mark IV 1D
that could capture 10 frames per second and 121 frames in a row without
having to stop and breathe. My camera equipment was nicer than the
statewide newspaper guy's, so the newspaper started paying me for my
photos instead of sending their own photographer. I got to stand on the
sideline and take pictures of my own kid and get paid for it.

Score!

But Ben's senior year was one for the record books in both football and track. He had worked extremely hard during summer workouts to get his weight up to 160 pounds while at the same time bringing his 40-yard dash time to under 4.4 seconds.

One of the football dads paid to bring in a foul-mouthed local dude who everyone seemed to admire for his training ability to handle the team's summer workout program. Apparently this guy played college ball some 15 years prior, played in Canada a couple of years, made four tackles for some XFL team one year, was later signed by an Arena Football team, and then got cut the very next day. But all I remember about him is four cuss words coming out of this dude's mouth for every five words he spoke. The kids thought he was cool; I thought he was a despicable fool. I guess the school administrators at our Christian school chose not to have an opinion.

Anyway, Ben chose to work hard, and went into his senior football season ready to run, and ready to run fast.

The first home football game Ben's senior year was against the Magnolia Heights Chiefs. The pre-game coin toss ceremony took a few minutes longer than normal to honor one of the Chief's fallen teammates. Just nine weeks earlier, 17-year-old Drew Bouchillon was severely injured while bush hogging a field in Como, Mississippi. Drew was thrown from his tractor and into the path of the bush hog. His lower back was injured and his legs were mutilated to the point that both had to be amputated. As Drew lay in the field, having lost most of the blood in his body, the tractor continued to make a wide circle, coming closer and closer to him with each pass. Ricky Armstrong looked out across the field and noticed the driverless tractor while passing by in his Panola County garbage truck.

He and jail trustees, Derek Joslin and Terry Potts, looked closer to see Drew holding his arm up in the field and were able to stop the tractor before it made its final fatal pass.

On game day Friday morning, Drew was continuing physical therapy at a Jackson hospital. He begged those in charge of his care to allow him to attend the coin toss. So when the first Friday Night Lights of the season flooded the Madison-Ridgeland Academy Patriot field that night, Drew was pushed across the 50-yard line in his wheelchair as an honorary team captain, much to the delight of teary-eyed parents and fans on both sides of the field.

Then it was game time.

Both teams were amped up and ready to play. The Chiefs won the coin toss, and after receiving the kickoff the MRA Patriot defense shut down the Chiefs after three downs and forced them to punt the football. MRA took their first home possession of the season on the Chief's 48-yard line. JT Williamson, MRA's play-by-play radio announcer, called it like this, "Ben Hutton your tailback, Myhan will go underneath center, three wide outs in the Patriot I formation. Self your up back, Hutton again your tailback, quick pitch to Hutton, trying to get to the corner, cuts it back to the inside, and Hutton may be gone to the house, Hutton on the left side, he's got one man to beat, TOUCHDOWN MRA from the first play of scrimmage!"

JT would call Ben's name 249 other times his senior year. By the end of the season, Ben had amassed 1,444 yards on 250 carries averaging 5.8 yards per carry. He averaged 125.3 yards per game and had a game high 232 yards against the St. Andrews Saints. Ben ran for 13 touchdowns, which included an 82-yard run and a 92-yard kickoff return. He had over 2,200 all purpose yards his senior year, over 4,000 career all purpose yards, and averaged over 7.5 yards whenever he touched the ball.

His 1,444 yards was a new single season rushing record for the MRA Patriots. He also was selected first team all county (of both public and private schools), first team all conference, and first team all state. He was voted 16 WAPT player of the week, twice selected the Clarion Ledger (statewide newspaper) player of the week, and chosen to represent the South on the Mississippi All-Star Football team where he scored an 80-yard touchdown the first time he touched the ball. His senior season ended, however, in a tear filled locker room much like he witnessed two years earlier as MRA lost the state championship game to Jackson Prep. Ben scored two touchdowns in that state championship game--the only two touchdowns scored against the Jackson Prep team the entire year.

Even so, some people would contend that as impressive as his senior year football statistics were, his senior year track statistics might have been even more impressive.

Ben was undefeated in every race he entered.

From the first track meet of the year through the state championship meet, he usually won by unbelievable margins. He ran in 27 races that spring of 2009 and took home 27 gold medals. He was named to the Clarion Ledger all state track team. He was the 100-meter state champion with 10.81 (just 4/100 seconds off the state record of 10.77). He was the 200-meter state champion setting a state record of 21.98. He was the anchor leg of the state champion 4x100 relay team, and the anchor leg of the state champion 4x200 relay team with a state record time of 43.20, which still holds today.

He graduated with decent grades, and Daddy rewarded him with an even nicer jacked-up Chevy Silverado LTZ. This truck had hydraulic running boards, DVD player, covered bed, matching fender flares, and a dozen other custom options. But Ben didn't pay a dime for any of it.

While every high school football player has visions of continuing their career in a big Division I football program, not too many 5'8", 160-pound private school ball carriers get that opportunity.

But Ben did.

Larry Fedora was the coach of the University of Southern Mississippi Golden Eagles, the same school I watched every fall growing up in Hattiesburg, Mississippi. USM was also the same school where I met my bride in the fall of 1983. Fedora, now head coach for the North Carolina Tarheels, builds his teams around speed, speed, and more speed. Ben had been officially clocked running a 4.27 40-yard dash. Fedora knew that a slot receiver with that kind of speed could find a few places to get open on the football field. So Fedora offered Ben a preferred walk-on spot, which means he was guaranteed a spot on the 105-man Division I roster. When we went to USM for Ben's official school visit, Coach Fedora's staff was just finishing up their first year on campus, so Joni and I ended up showing them around more than they showed us around. We showed Ben the buildings where we had our classes, the field where the fraternity house once stood where Joni and I first met, and the library I had to run past naked one night after my fraternity brothers stripped me down after Joni and I were ceremonially "pinned."

Ben would begin college immediately in June so he could participate in summer workouts with his new Golden Eagle teammates. Ben's locker was just a few spaces down from the glass-encased locker of #4 Brett Favre. He took two classes that summer to get a head start on his academics. In one team meeting, Coach Fedora called a select few players to the front of the room. Ben was one of those called. He thought he was in trouble or maybe had broken a team rule, but instead Coach Fedora revealed to the rest of the team those players who had a 4.0 GPA that summer semester.

WJTV, the Jackson CBS affiliate, did a nice story on the little man going to the big school. WAPT, the Jackson ABC affiliate also did a story that summer. In addition, Ben was once again mentioned in a nice write-up in the statewide newspaper.

Ben's name would also appear in our local newspaper.

The Madison County Jail Docket appears on Thursdays, usually 7-10 days after a person's arrest. Ben was arrested for his first DUI that summer. His explanation was that he had been the designated driver all night for some of his friends, and had simply had a beer at 2:00 a.m. after his duties were complete. But then one more person needed a quick ride, and since he had just had the one beer, he obliged.

This was my first 2:00 a.m. phone call, the first of about 20 over the next few years. The infraction occurred just a couple of blocks from our house, and the deputy was nice enough to call me and let me come pick up Ben's vehicle to save me the towing charges. After a couple of good years finishing up high school and after a good start at USM, my first thought was not *Is this the beginning of a problem* or *Do we need to set an appropriate punishment,* but instead my first thought was *I wonder if this will cause any problem with Coach Fedora?*

I'm just being honest--my first real thought was about how it would affect Ben's football career.

Chapter 7

Pride  Aside

*Yes, we are fully confident, and we would rather
be away from these bodies, for then we will be at
home with the Lord.* (2 CORINTHIANS 5:8, NLT)

Death is a sobering experience for the family and friends of the one who
is no longer on this Earth. I didn't experience much death in my growing
up years. Neither did Joni. When I was in high school, there were three
young men at a neighboring school who were killed in a car accident.
One of those young men and I had gone to church and Sunday School
together when we were in elementary school. We also played on the same
church basketball team, but I didn't really keep up with him once we got
to middle school. He was someone I knew, but not a close friend. Beyond
them, and a grandparent passing away, I didn't really know much about
death.

Ben had already experienced tragedy close up and personal by this
time in his life. Scott Lloyd was a great friend to Ben. They went to
separate schools, but Scott lived in a neighboring subdivision and spent
a great deal of time at our house. One summer, Scott probably slept at
our house more than he did at his own house. Though Ben's passion was
football, and Scott's passion was baseball, both of them enjoyed playing
golf occasionally. They loved to spend summer afternoons playing golf
together at the country club.

One afternoon, Scott and two of his friends had a couple of free hours after school, before their evening baseball game at Canton Academy, a smaller private school in the town north of Madison. Like most small town boys, riding around in one of their vehicles was the activity of choice. Not too far from our neighborhood and Scott's neighborhood is a stretch of road known as "thrill hill." I think there are a lot of communities with a thrill hill. When visiting my grandparents in Missouri we would go rainbow trout fishing at Roaring River State Park, and would travel over Southwest Missouri's version of thrill hill during the six-mile trek from my grandparents' house to the river. It was a little hilltop in the middle of the Ozark Mountains with several wreaths and crosses on the side of the road remembering those who once sought a thrill and did not survive.

You know what thrill hill is, right?

It is a section of road with a pretty sharp peak. When you're driving, if your vehicle is going fast enough, you can lose your stomach a little bit when topping the crest. As you drive up the hill you get that roller coaster experience. You can see where the road disappears at the top of the crest while inching closer and closer. The illusion of not being able to see the other side, coupled with the actual feeling of the vehicle going up and then suddenly going down, maybe even "catching some air" as the teenagers say, gives a person the feeling their stomach has gone through their throat and left their body completely. A fast moving elevator or jumping off of a high dive might give you the same sensation, but thrill hill will do it every time.

On that afternoon before the baseball game, I guess Scott wanted to see how far he could push the envelope. Zach Bailey and Mitch Dickens were along for the ride. Scott hit the peak of thrill hill at apparently a very high rate of speed and his truck may have become airborne. Once on the other side of the hill he couldn't regain control before leaving the road and slamming into a tree. Instantly three young men lost their lives.

I remember that day.

Ben ran out of the house and was texting on his phone as he headed for his truck. I was only able to get a short word from him: "Scott's been in a wreck." The only advice I could give in the three seconds before he drove off was, "Hey, go slow. You getting there faster won't make the wreck go away. I am sure everything is fine."

It was not. That was Ben's first experience with death. But he was going to experience more death, much more death, over the next few years.

The fall of 2009 began with football camp at Southern Miss. Coach Fedora never learned about Ben's DUI, so Ben never got in any trouble with the university or the team. In Division I football, there are a multitude of rules about how many days a player can practice, how many hours a player can practice per day, what constitutes a countable hour, and on and on. Countable hours versus non-countable hours is very interesting stuff, as is voluntary activity versus countable activities. For instance, required weight training is countable; voluntary weight training is not. Reviewing game film is countable but training room, medical treatment, and rehab activities are not. Meetings initiated or required by a coach are countable while meetings initiated by the student athlete are not. In spring practice a team is allowed to have 15 practice sessions within a period of 34 consecutive calendar days. Only 12 may include physical contact but none of the 12 can happen in the first two practice days. Tackling is allowed in eight of the twelve contact sessions; up to three of those eight tackling sessions may be devoted to 11-on-11 scrimmages. The spring game counts as one of the three scrimmage days.

Then there is "camp."

Prior to the first game of the season, a team must count backwards to the day they may begin camp by choosing a date that allows 40 units of practice. Each day represents one or two units as specified by the NCAA, and a team may not have more than 29 on-field practice sessions during the pre-season.

Division I Bowl Subdivision schools are allowed to have 105 student-athletes who may practice before the first day of classes or the first game, whichever comes first. There might be 150 football players on a school's roster, but only the 105 are considered the official roster. The other players beyond the 105 are often referred to as the scout team or practice squad. These young men dress out during practice like the following week's opposing team, they line up like the other team, run plays like the other team, and generally pretend to be the other team in order to simulate the play of future opponents. Of the 105 on the roster, 85 are on scholarship and 20 are preferred walk-ons who usually end up on scholarship the following year if they maintain their place on the depth chart. Among the 105, there is no differentiation between scholarship and preferred walk-on players. The best man at a position plays that position.

Ben was excited but nervous about being in the 105 and about starting camp. Physically it was nothing, as he was in terrific shape. But he had been moved to slot receiver, which was outside his comfort zone. And there was another issue. About 90 percent of all the kids in our town go to either the University of Mississippi (Ole Miss) or to Mississippi State University. Probably all of Ben's friends went to one of those colleges. So Ben found himself at a school he had never admired growing up, in a town that was unfamiliar, with literally no friends. Overall, he was not too happy.

Just nine days into camp, an old shoulder injury flared up. Ben decided to have surgery again and "redshirt" that season. Redshirt simply means you do not take the field that year. That one-year of eligibility does not count against you and you still have four more seasons to play ball. I think he would admit today that the injury probably didn't require surgery and sitting out a year. But the combination of feeling out of place on the team, not really wanting to be at the school, and having to fight through rehab made the decision easy. He could blame the injury, have surgery, and sit out with a good medical excuse. By doing so, he found himself even further on the outside looking in. He stood on the sidelines of practice and watched. He was not allowed to take the field for games. He even had to get a ticket to the first home game just like any other student.

He did, however, hit it off with one young man right from the start. Peter Wilkes was from Union City, Tennessee. Peter, along with his dad, the Rev. Ben Wilkes, a retired minister, and his mom, Kay, were visiting the USM campus in early June where Peter was going to walk-on as a Golden Eagle punter. With Peter the son and Kay the wife sitting idly in their hotel room, Ben the father had a heart attack and died. After the funeral, Peter and his family decided that his dad would want him to continue his dream so Peter returned to Hattiesburg for the fall semester.

That fall, Ben and Peter spent a good deal of time together. They talked a lot about their mutual sadness--of Peter's loss of his father and of Ben's feeling of not being where he really wanted to be. Ben also began to use his prescribed painkillers in a non-prescribed way. He used the pills not only to dull the pain of his shoulder but also just to dull his pain. Both boys were depressed. Peter was worried about Ben, but Ben was really worried about Peter.

If the aforementioned NCAA rules were not confusing enough about who is on the team, how much they can practice, and who gets scholarships and who does not, the conference travel guidelines add even another layer of complexity. While there are 105 players on the roster, and while 105 players may dress out for a home game, in Conference USA (where the Southern Miss Golden Eagles participate) only 66 players are allowed on a conference game travel squad. So not all 105 make the road trips. Usually a team will look at a variety of factors and determine how many quarterbacks or running backs or defensive ends they want to have travel that week. Almost always there is just one punter or one kicker to travel. Peter Wilkes was not going to be traveling to Louisville, Kentucky for the October game against the University of Louisville, so he decided to go home and visit his family that weekend. His family was going to use that opportunity to pick out a headstone for the father's final resting place.

Ben was worried about some of the things Peter had been communicating both verbally and non-verbally throughout the fall. Once Ben asked him, "Are you going to kill yourself?"

Peter told him "No."

While at home that weekend, Peter had been sitting at the kitchen table with a close friend after a long, fun day together. His older brother had just gone upstairs when a gun they had been target practicing with earlier in the day went off and struck Peter in the head. Whether Peter intended to kill himself we will never know. Still, Ben lost a good friend once again. He helped clean out Peter's apartment and traveled to Union City to take part in the funeral per the family's request.

I remember taking Ben to buy him a new black suit, which was probably his only suit. I also remember something not being right that day. It's normal that someone would be emotional after losing a friend, but there was something deeper. Ben was confused, agitated, pale, distracted, and depressed. I would estimate he weighed about 145 pounds, his hair was long, and he was unshaven. He just looked like garbage. This wasn't something that had occurred just in the two days since Peter's death. Again, another warning sign was staring me in the face. But as a parent, how do you ever concede the fact that your child may be on a destructive path? When you look at your children you want to see the best in them; you want to see their hopes and aspirations come to fruition right before your eyes. You want to see them happy with their future mate and happy with their future children and happy in their future career. You just want to picture them as happy. You never, at least not early on, can look at your children and picture them in rehab after rehab, moving from one sober living facility to another, relapsing, running, chasing, hiding, fighting, and slowly dying. Instead, you look at them and picture your baby. Or you picture them when they were two years old pushing a toy lawnmower behind you in the yard while you push the real thing.

Wow, the toy lawnmower!

That was my favorite toy that we ever bought Ben when he was little. I doubt he has any actual memories of the lawnmower, other than what he has seen in pictures. As a young PGA professional in Ruston, I kept the lawn on our first house manicured like a golf course. It was the house Ben first lived in as a newborn. I mowed the entire yard every Monday, which was my day off. I also mowed the front yard again every Thursday, the day I usually came home around 5:00 p.m. Ben was just learning how to walk, and he would come out to the front yard and push his toy lawnmower behind me as I pushed my Snapper self-propelled in front of him. Honest to goodness, Ben's first word he ever spoke was "lawnmower." Before he ever said Mama or DaDa, he looked at Joni one day while pointing through the front window at me mowing the yard and said, "Mawmowa."

A couple of weeks after Peter's funeral, Ben called and talked to me a little bit about how he was unhappy at USM. He really wanted to look into transferring to another school.

Again, with perfect hindsight, I now can see this was a very consistent pattern Ben would repeat over and over and over again for several years. Ben would quit, move, change locations, or just run away from whatever hurdle he was facing. Looking back, this was the second instance of him running away from tough situations, but it would take a few more before I would pick up on it. The first was shoulder surgery. While his shoulder was in pain, the coaches and physical therapists told him it was not a season-ending condition and he could complete his first season, then have surgery during the winter. But for Ben it was an opportunity to run away from the hard work and discomfort he would have to endure to succeed.

The fall of 2009 was when Ben started using drugs for more than recreation. Drugs had also become a way to escape from uncertainty. To have a successful fall, Ben was going to have to wake up early every day, spend time in weight training and conditioning, go to class, eat lunch, go to athletic study hall, go to football practice, eat dinner, study, go to sleep when normal people go to sleep, wake up early, and repeat. This was the discipline it would take to see the season through to the end. But instead he chose surgery, painkillers, going to bed late, sleeping late, and attending the fewest classes he could attend and still get by. He would then make an appearance at practice so the coaches would see him before he slipped off. Then he would repeat it all the next day.

Ben's desire to leave and go to another school was the beginning of a pattern. It was a pattern that led to a constant feeling of failure, then a constant desire to start over.

Again and again, he would repeat the pattern.

But as we talked on the phone that day, I didn't have the luxury of hindsight. I didn't see the repeating pattern. I only had the facts that were presented to me at the time. So my reply to him was, "Ben, you know I love you, and will support you. You can go to any school in this country and I will help you…as long as it's not Ole Miss."

Chapter 8

Pride  Aside

When I was a child, I talked like a child, I thought
like a child, I reasoned like a child. When I became
a man I put the ways of childhood behind me.
(1 CORINTHIANS 13:11, NIV)

In the fall of 2007, Coach Houston Nutt of the Arkansas Razorbacks was under fire from the fans and alumni around The Natural State. Nutt had compiled a respectable record of 75-48 over his 10-year head coaching stint in Fayetteville. This record placed him second on the all time win list behind Frank Broyles, who was more like Razorback royalty than simply a former coach.

Just one year before his dismissal from Arkansas, the football faithful were full of woooooo-pig-soooeeee's every time Nutt brought his team onto the Frank Broyles Field at the Donald W. Reynolds Razorback Stadium. The Razorbacks lost their 2006 home opener to USC, but went on a ten game tear after that game. Led at quarterback by local Springdale prodigy Mitch Mustain, the winning streak that followed included toppling #22 Alabama at home and #2 Auburn on the road. Mustain's high school coach was Gus Malzahn, who seemed to come to Arkansas as offensive coordinator that year as somewhat of a package deal with Mustain. The Razorbacks won two out of their last four games that season including a win over 13th ranked Tennessee. Though ranked #7 in the BCS standings, Arkansas lost their final regular season game to the neighboring rival #8 LSU Tigers. Even so, they were the Western Division Champions of the SEC that year. Despite losing the SEC Championship to the 4th ranked Florida Gators and losing the New Year's Day Capital One Bowl to the #5 Wisconsin Badgers, Nutt was named SEC coach of the year by the Associated Press and by the SEC coaches for the second time.

But oh what a difference a year can make.

The 2007 preseason AP poll had Nutt's Razorbacks ranked #21. Things looked good after their victory in a home opener against Troy. But early season losses to Alabama and Kentucky knocked Arkansas out of the rankings and the rest of the SEC schedule was a struggle as well. Fans soon forgot the joy of the 2006 season, some began wearing all black to the games, and many displayed anti-Nutt sentiments. Blogs were written with hate filled, anti-Nutt rants, full-page ads in Arkansas newspapers called for his head, and a small plane flew over the stadium prior to the Auburn home game pulling a banner that read: "Fire Houston Nutt. Players and fans deserve better."

I was relaxing at deer camp with my friend David Thames on the day after Thanksgiving as the Razorbacks went to Tiger Stadium to take on the #1 team in the country, their bitter rival the LSU Tigers. Many surmised it would be Nutt's last regular season game as the Arkansas head coach. Surely the Tigers would embarrass the Razorbacks on national television then Nutt would be gone. My luck on predicting football outcomes has never been very good, but that afternoon I made a prognostication that would prove to be true.

I predicted that Arkansas would upset LSU, but they would fire Nutt anyway. I also predicted that the Ole Miss Rebels would lose their end of the season rivalry game to the Mississippi State Bulldogs, and Ole Miss would terminate Ed Orgeron after three disappointing years. Then, to complete the trifecta, I predicted that Ole Miss, who for years had tried to scrape by hiring those they thought to be up-and-coming coaches, would reach deep in their pockets and bring in the veteran Houston Nutt.

Well on that weekend the Razorbacks won, the Rebels lost, Orgeron was dismissed from Ole Miss, Nutt was fired (or forced to resign) from Arkansas, and then just a few days later Nutt was named the head coach at Ole Miss.

Hotty Toddy.

Nutt's first two years in Oxford, Mississippi were just what the Rebel Nation was hoping for. They had back-to-back Cotton Bowl wins and finished the seasons ranked #14 and #20, respectively, in the AP poll. The Rebels were on a roll.

I called the strength and conditioning coach at Ole Miss, Don Decker, who was a friend of a friend. I told him the whole ugly truth about Ben's experience at USM, except I left out the part about the painkillers. I told him about the good grades, the surgery, the friend's death, and the desire to be anywhere other than at USM. I drove to Oxford and had lunch with Don. I took him Ben's high school game films and a resume listing all of his stats. I painted a picture of a great kid with a big heart who had lost hope both from injury and the death of a friend, and who just needed a fresh start. Don arranged a time for Ben and I to meet with Coach Nutt in early December of 2009 to talk about possibly transferring to Ole Miss.

But I began to get that sick feeling again.

I really did not think going to Ole Miss was the right thing for Ben, and neither did Joni. I wondered, *Why am I going to all this trouble to pave the way for his transfer?* Maybe my disdain for Ole Miss was because I was raised in Hattiesburg, Mississippi, brought up a Southern Miss fan, and had been taught at an early age to "dislike" the Rebels of Ole Miss. In a fun, joking, rivalry kind of way, of course. In the 1970s and 80s, Ole Miss would play USM as a part of their non-conference schedule. USM would beat Ole Miss quite often, and eventually the Rebels ended the rivalry. I think in the sixth grade I actually thought the last line of the national anthem was "go to (bad word) Ole Miss," because it was screamed at every Southern Miss home game right after we sang, "O'er the land of the free, and the home of the brave."

But put all of that silly football rivalry stuff aside.

Ben was in bad shape physically, emotionally, and spiritually. He had no idea what he wanted to major in or what career to pursue. Most students have some sort of idea what they want to study in college. Or if they don't know for sure, most at least are going for the right reasons and figure it out within their first year or so of school. But some are there for the wrong reason--they just want to get away from home.

As an aside, if your son or daughter does not know what major they want to pursue, then why do they initially need to go to college? College is designed to get a four-year academic degree in a specific field of study so the graduate can enter the work force and make more money than someone who enters the same work force without a college education. So if a young man or woman does not know what he or she wants to do, then a great alternative would be to go get a stinking job for a year or two, start paying their own car note, start paying their own phone bill, start paying their own insurance, and if they ever figure out what they want to study, THEN they can go to college.

So many kids today have a different plan, at least those in our community who are suffering from the disease of "affluenza." Their plan is to go to college, take classes they care nothing about, join a fraternity or sorority, ride on their parents payroll as long as possible, and have as much fun as they can until their parents finally force them to pick a major so they can graduate and move on. Then after a few years of hating that job and developing an interest in a different field, can they go back to school and start over on their dime.

Sorry, I got to preaching there for a second!

Anyway, I did not feel good about Ben's move at all; WE did not feel good about it. Ole Miss is a great school and produces some of the sharpest graduates Mississippi has to offer. I really didn't feel right about Ben going to any college at that point, much less the school that for years had been consistently listed as one of the top five party schools in the nation. But I found myself beginning the vicious cycle of trying to help Ben find happiness. I felt if I could help make things better for him, then he would be happy, and if he became happy again he would then have the drive and determination to succeed.

Let me write that out for you again in case you missed it.

I felt if I could help make things better for him, then he would be happy, and if he became happy again he would then have the drive and determination to succeed.

Now let me preach one more time.

I now realize it was not my job to make things easy for Ben so he could be happy. It was my job to help prepare him to become a man, which may or may not immediately bring happiness. I was to model for him what it looked like to be a man, and in our home, that meant a Christian man. He was to provide for his family, and at age 18 he was a family of one. So he was to provide for himself. He was to find one woman whom he would marry and be with forever. He was to provide for her and their children. Now if that meant going to college and studying hard to prepare for a career, then I was good with that and was very willing to support him financially. If he was able to make good grades and still have time to enjoy an athletic hobby, then I was good with that. But here I was making phone calls to friends of friends to manipulate a meeting with a college football coach for the sole purpose of helping him find a way to play football in college.

So we met with Coach Nutt.

Ben wore an oversized hoodie sweatshirt so it would not be immediately apparent that he weighed barely over 150 pounds. His shoulder was mostly healed and he had just started lifting weights again. He was also starting to add back a few pounds.

Here are some more NCAA rules for you.

If a player transfers from a Division I school to another Division I school, he usually has to sit out a year before being eligible to play in a game. He can practice and he can be a part of the team, but he cannot suit up on Saturday. I decided to search the rules for any exceptions and I found a few. There were family emergency exceptions, which did not apply. There was one exception that seemed to fit Ben's situation. If a player transferred to a school that did not recruit him (which Ole Miss did not), and he participated less than 14 days at the school he transferred from (surgery occurred day nine of camp at USM), then he did not have to sit out a year. The compliance department at both Ole Miss and

Southern Miss agreed. He was cleared to transfer and would become immediately eligible to play. So even though I thought surgery during preseason camp was a bad idea, ironically it paid off for Ben.

Let me say this--I really like Houston Nutt.

I just do. My dad is a Razorback fan. He and my mom retired to Northwest Arkansas so they could be near his beloved university where he received his PhD in Psychology in 1968. He liked Houston Nutt also. At least he did until two years ago when as a dedicated Razorback fan he was supposed to join the bandwagon and hate Houston Nutt. Even so I really liked the guy. He made Ben feel special. He praised Ben for his high school career and said he loved watching his high school game film.

I even liked the way this guy spoke.

He spoke in short, choppy sentences. He is well-known as a great motivational speaker. He knows how to use rhythm and cadence in his voice and knows how to deliver a punch line with perfect timing. I know he is somewhat full of bull, but I admire how he can be both full of bull and believable at the same time. He said, "Ben, you can't teach speed. You've got speed. I need speed. I need lots of speed. You've got speed. I need you to be an Ole Miss Rebel. Dexter McCluster just graduated and will be in the 2010 NFL draft. I need to replace Dexter. Can you replace Dexter? I can see you taking a direct snap in the Wild Rebel formation. Ben, I want you to come here this spring and become an Ole Miss Rebel. We won the Cotton Bowl last year. We are going to the Cotton Bowl again this year. Do you want to go to the Cotton Bowl with us? I can get you some tickets. Can you start school in January? Can you be with us for spring practice? I need you here, Ben. I need speed. You've got speed. I need you to become an Ole Miss Rebel."

After those words from Coach Nutt, you would have thought Ben just signed a $10 million contract after being named a first round draft pick in the NFL. He was happy. And once again I had succeeded: I worked my contacts, made the right calls, and put him where he wanted to be.

But I didn't feel right about any of it.

Chapter 9

Pride  Aside

But when these things begin to take place,
straighten up and lift up your heads, because your
redemption is drawing near.
(Luke 21:28, NASB)

Coach Nutt was without question full of bull, but again, I still really
liked the guy. His embellishments were not meant for harm. Instead,
they were intended to help his players dream big, feel confident, and see
positive things in themselves that could only make them better athletes,
better students, and better persons. In addition to being known by
numerous coaching awards such as the SEC Coach of the Year in 2001,
2006, and 2008, Nutt was also a Christian. He was not ashamed to share
his love of Christ with his fellow coaches and players. On January 13,
2010 the Hutton household was getting things ready for Ben to move
to Oxford and start spring conditioning workouts the following week.
That same day Nutt was in Orlando receiving the 2009 FCA (Fellowship
of Christian Athletes) Grant Teaff Coach of the Year Award. On the
platform with him was retired Indianapolis Colts coach and Super Bowl
winner Tony Dungy receiving the FCA Grant Teaff Lifetime Achievement
Award.

Nutt was generous with his time and money.

He and his wife Diana gave back to the community in Oxford in a variety of ways. They gave $100,000 to the University of Mississippi to create scholarships for deserving student athletes and to help build the Indoor Practice Facility. Nutt was a "player's coach," meaning he invested in the lives of the players. He invited them to his house, he loved on them, and he took a genuine interest in their lives and cared for their well-being on and off the field. He also hired coaches who did the same.

Don Decker is the most amazing football coach I have ever met. His list of accomplishments as a strength and conditioning coach is long and distinguished. He earned the designation of master level strength coach by the Collegiate Strength and Conditioning Coaches Association, one of just 70-such coaches in the world as of 2004. But I believe Decker could just as easily have been a pastor of a church. While walking in the Indoor Practice Facility with him one day, he stopped players he met, looked them in the eye, and asked them questions that showed he genuinely cared about them. He knew what was going on in their lives, both on and off the field. He would ask about their girlfriends, about their families, and about a variety of subjects beyond football.

This huge man who looked more like Mr. Universe than a coach would hug them, not just high five them, and sometimes pray with them. For the first four weeks or so of Ben's time on campus, Decker was Ben's coach, not Nutt. It was Decker's job to get the players ready for spring football workouts before turning them over to the position coaches. The one good feeling I had about leaving Ben in Oxford was knowing that Don Decker was going to be invested in his life, both on and off campus.

But another red flag was soon to be waved in front of my eyes, and again I would do nothing about it.

The coaching staff made arrangements for Ben to live in the Honors Dorm. Several of the players lived there. It was newer, the rooms were nicer, and food was better. Ben was assigned a roommate, Cameron Whigham, a 6-3, 255 pound Defensive End transfer from Snellville, Georgia. Cameron became a four-year letterman and put up some impressive numbers. But Ben did not want to live with the football players. He wanted to live with an old high school friend in a regular dorm so he could have a life outside of football. This was the red flag I ignored.

If you are a student athlete, especially a football player, there is no life outside of class and football.

If you are not in class or studying, you are at practice or watching film. If you are not at practice or watching film, you are in class or studying. It's what you signed up for and it's what is expected. It's also what it takes to be a good student and a good athlete. Ben, however, thought he could add a third element to his life: partying with old friends. But to add this element one of the others would suffer--either studies or athletics.

In Ben's case, it ended up being both.

For a while Ben's workouts were going well. His weight was approaching 160 pounds again. He was getting his strength back and he was impressing the coaches with his speed and agility. The coaches had the players doing some running drills early one morning before class as part of their conditioning. The coaches would call out two players of similar size and position, like two offensive guards or two wide receivers, and pit them against each other for speed trial. They would run several yards down the field, bend down and touch a line, run back, touch a line, run again down the field, touch a line, then sprint back. This tested them both in a flat out sprint situation and also from an agility standpoint.

Cars are often measured in how fast they can go from 0-60 mph, which measures the car's explosiveness. Athletes are tested in a similar fashion.

Ben's name was called and he was paired with Korvic Neat, a 5'9" 166 pound receiver from Hallandale, Florida. Korvic already had one year under his belt as an Ole Miss Rebel. In addition he had established himself as the fastest player on the team. Both Ben and Korvic were small, thin, agile, and fast. The whistle blew and it was on, the established fastest guy on the team head to head with the new guy who was showing promise. When the two made the last turn for the final sprint, Ben was already well in the lead, and he pulled away even further over the final few yards. The surrounding players started yelling and whooping. Their actions were partially a friendly jab at Korvic--letting him know there was new kid in town--and partly in praise for Ben for working hard, stepping up, and showing his stuff. The coaches joined in on the accolades. So Ben felt like he fit in, like he could contribute, like he was an Ole Miss Rebel.

My cell phone rang twice that morning.

The first phone call I got was from Ben. He was pumped. He told me the story and I could tell he felt encouraged and empowered. The second phone call I got was from Don Decker and Houston Nutt who were both on speakerphone. They both went on and on about Ben's speed, and especially relayed how Ben went up against Korvic and came out on top.

A few days later I received another phone call from Don Decker. This one, however, was not quite so affirming. Decker had received a weekly report of each player's class attendance history. If a player missed a class, his name was on the list. The coaching staff at Ole Miss placed a very high priority on attending class, attending study hall, working with tutors, and placing academics above all else. For the staff, playing football was a privilege while going to class was an obligation. Ben had already missed three days of class just a couple of weeks into school. I remember Decker saying, "What is this kid thinking? I cannot have him showing up on any lists. I went out on a limb to get him in here, and he repays me by showing up on a list?"

I drove up to meet with Ben and Decker, and Decker laid down the law. We also met with Ben's position coach, Derrick Nix, who was entering his third year as the Rebel's running back coach. Nix also had a distinguished playing career as a Golden Eagle at Southern Miss. He was the first Golden Eagle to rush for 1,000 yards in each of his freshman and sophomore seasons and the only Eagle and Conference USA player ever to rush for 1,000 yards or more in three seasons. Nix took us to a facility I didn't even know existed. Ben didn't know about it either, which was odd because he was supposed to be going there every day.

The FedEx Student-Athlete Academic and Support Center was incredible! FedEx had given Ole Miss $2.5 million to help create an elite academic support center solely for student-athletes. This 22,500 square foot facility included conference rooms, 20 large and small group-tutoring rooms, a large study area, a multi media classroom, a computer lab with dozens of workstations and computers, and a 150-seat high-tech auditorium. The total price tag for the facility was $5 million. It was built as a sanctuary for all the student athletes on campus to help them concentrate on academics. The FedEx Center was located right beside the football stadium and the Indoor Practice Facility. A student athlete could go to class, go to practice, and then walk over to the FedEx Center to study or meet with tutors.

In addition to skipping class, Ben had never walked through the doors of this facility either. Thus his name was on a list, a bad list, which made the coaches very unhappy. The Senior Associate Athletics Director for Academic Support was waiting for Coach Nix, Ben, and me after we toured the facility. She looked at Ben when she first laid eyes on him and provided the following snide, condescending thought:

"So THIS is Ben Hutton. Nice to meet you finally."

My stomach turned with embarrassment, but it was nothing like the embarrassment I would experience in the future. She told Ben that a football player missing one class brought a warning. Missing two classes meant the player lost his four complimentary tickets for friends and family to attend the football games. But when the player missed three classes, he wouldn't get the opportunity to suit up and play in the first two games of the next year's season. She overlooked his offenses since he had not gone through any type of new student orientation like players who entered school in the fall. But she made it very clear that the reason he was at Ole Miss was for academics. She said she couldn't care less if he ever played football.

In that meeting I recognized something interesting about Ole Miss, which I had not observed with other schools. Other schools probably used the same vernacular, but for some reason I had not noticed. No one at this school ever used the term "football player." Instead, they only used the term "student athlete." What Ben realized then was that he could only live two lives if he wanted to be a student athlete: the life of a student and the life of an athlete. Thus he had a decision to make. Would he give up the third life he was trying to live? This was the life that quite honestly he wanted to live more than the other two--a life of friends, booze, drugs, parties, late nights, and sleeping in. In his mind, he thought he could do all three.

But he was wrong.

On Friday, February 19, Ben and all of the players arrived early at the Indoor Practice Facility. After one month of conditioning and training, they were about to go through a ritual the coaches called 4th quarter.

As you may know, most football games are won or lost in the 4th quarter. Both teams begin the game fresh and ready to play. For three quarters players often match up well against each other: stride for stride and strength against strength. But the better team usually emerges in the 4th quarter. It's a matter of which team has the greater desire to win. It's also a factor of which team conditioned and disciplined themselves to play until the last whistle was blown.

The 4th quarter workout at Ole Miss was built around 10 workstations. It was designed to exhaust the players of their strength and test their longevity and sustainability. One young player was about to fail that test, and he would never have an opportunity to be tested again.

Bennie Abrams, Ben's assigned workout partner, was a 20-year-old, 5'9" 186 pound safety from Southaven, Mississippi. Bennie had completed a two-year stint at Itawamba Junior College where he received an Associates Degree with honors before transferring to Ole Miss the previous fall. For four weeks Ben and Bennie ran together, lifted together, spotted each other, and got to know each other. But just 15 minutes into the 4th quarter workout that morning, Bennie collapsed at the first station. At the urging of the coaching staff, Bennie resumed his workout, and collapsed again at the second station. Bennie was then sent to the sideline to rest while the other players completed the remaining drills. The coaches soon realized Bennie was still in a state of distress and had him transported to the local hospital, where he died. It was later learned that Bennie had tested positive for Sickle Cell Trait, and his death came from exertion leading to Cardiomegaly, an enlarged heart.

For the third time, death hit close to home for Ben.

But that day it hit even harder for the Ole Miss coaches, staff, and trainers. They were completely devastated by Bennie's death and many of them questioned what role they might have played. Did the staff know from Bennie's sports physical that he possessed the sickle cell trait (SCT), and that the NCAA had certain guidelines for dealing with athletes who suffered from the condition? That was unclear based on a lawsuit later filed by the family. Was the workout too hard? Probably not; it was vigorous, but players had endured it well in seasons past. Was his condition taken into account early enough by the coaching staff in determining when to get him to the hospital? Again it is unclear what the staff knew about the SCT issue. They did give him a few minutes to rest, and acted appropriately when they realized he was still in distress by having him transported to the hospital. Did the hospital physician, who was also the team physician, act appropriately? The answers to those questions may never be known. But what is certain is that an honor student athlete lost his life that day, and everyone associated with the team was left in shock.

Ben had a medical episode occur the following Monday morning during the team workouts. As you can imagine, there was no hesitation by the staff to act quickly. Ben had enjoyed his weekend; by this point both his weekdays and weekends included some form of drug use, alcohol consumption, or both.

A common occurrence on all college campuses today, and on most high school campuses as well, is the improper use of ADD (Attention Deficit Disorder) medication. Many kids coming out of high school, who have been prescribed ADD medicine, do not want to be on that medicine. But even students who are not prescribed the medicine like to take it when they need that extra level of concentration, or a boost in energy, perhaps to study for a test or just make it through class after a long night of partying. In my college days if you needed to stay up late you made a pot of coffee then ran the coffee back through the same grounds to make it stronger. We called it Cowboy Coffee. Some students also took NoDoz for added caffeine. But today, students who have prescriptions for ADD medicines are happy to sell the pills to students who do not for about $6 or $7 per pill. Thus they can get about $200 per month for a prescription their parents probably still pay for. I don't think parents today have any idea how many of their kids are taking ADD medicine that has been prescribed to another kid.

When our youngest son Michael was 14 years old, he went to a Civil Air Patrol Encampment in Panama City Beach for a week. Civil Air Patrol is the civilian auxiliary of the United States Air Force. It was a great taste for young people about what military life might be like. They woke up at 6:00 a.m., did calisthenics, wore a uniform, marched, did team building drills, and had a parade in review at the end of their week. Michael got sick during encampment and I had to go pick him up late one night, a couple of days before he was supposed to come home. As I prepared to leave, Ben's high school girlfriend, who we absolutely adored, without even thinking twice about it, said to me, "Mr. Steve, let me give you an Adderall to take with you in case you get sleepy driving." I replied that I did not realize she took ADD medicine. To which she replied, "Oh I don't, I just got some from a friend for when I need to study late." This truly is the norm with young people today.

They honestly do not think twice about it.

Ben loved to take Adderall or Vyvanse to get that extra boost when he needed it. Before his workout that Monday he thought taking two might be what he needed to wake up and make it through his morning workout. Much like Bennie, but for entirely different reasons, Ben collapsed and passed out in the weight room of the Indoor Practice Facility. He woke up with Don Decker on top of him, rubbing his knuckles along his sternum to try and jolt him back to consciousness. The coach was also praying out loud over Ben because he did not want to see another of his players die in front of him.

My cell phone rang. It was Coach Decker.

Don told me Ben had been taken to the hospital. This was the same hospital where Bennie had died three days earlier. Decker's voice was a mixture of pure panic and pure rage. He was somewhat in a panic because of what he had just endured as he tried to revive Ben, not knowing how serious it was. And he was still emotionally and physically exhausted from the events of the previous 72 hours with Bennie Abrams. But he was also mad, very mad. He couldn't understand how Ben could be so stupid to come to an SEC level workout having taken double the amount of prescription medicine not even prescribed to him! Or why he would choose to do it on the very next workout day after tragedy had just struck the team. The coach was rattled, scared, and furious. He said Coach Nutt wanted to see Ben and me in his office in a few days when he returned from an out of town trip. So I quickly got in my Yukon and headed to the hospital in Oxford. I would make that same 150-mile drive to Ole Miss several times over the next few months, and not a single trip would be for positive reasons.

I met Ben in the emergency room, where one of the training staff had been sitting with him. Again, the staff was so freaked out by the circumstances of the previous 72 hours they did not want to leave a player's side even though he was in a physician's care at the hospital. Ben's attitude was not remorseful or contrite, but rather defiant, like the whole incident was a big inconvenience. He just wanted to leave the hospital, and soon we were on our way.

He had a class coming up but he really did not want to go. His head was still foggy and hurting. He still felt nauseous from taking too much Adderall and maybe even from taking too much of whatever else over the weekend. His car was still at the Indoor Practice Facility, so I drove him to his first class. He had an hour break in between the first class and the second class, so I went back to pick him up but had to park a few buildings away. When I met him, he said he just wanted to go to sleep-- he didn't feel like going to any other classes that day. That set me off. Within seconds we were engaged in a cussing tirade on the sidewalks of The Grove at Ole Miss. I reminded him of the obvious about missing any more classes. He informed me that he did not give a (bad word), he felt sick, and he was going to sleep! Then he walked one way and I walked another. His agitation would become greater and greater with each similar episode we experienced over the next few years.

But I still remember that day in February as another benchmark moment for both of us: the cussing tirade.

Football was really over for Ben on that day.

They would not allow him to practice the rest of that week until we had a chance to talk to Coach Nutt, which we did. It was the typical "Did you learn your lesson" talk, followed by the "Are you ready to put it behind you and get back to work" question. Ben said he was. But he was not. After that week he went to practice a few more times, but soon I got a call from the Player Development Coach asking if I knew where Ben was. Ben was done. He simply quit a few days before the Spring Game. Coach Nutt had told me they had six plays picked out for Ben in the Spring Game, but he would never step foot on a game day field again after that day.

Chapter 10

Pride  Aside

But if you fail to do this, you will be sinning
against the Lord; and you may be sure that your sin
will find you out. (Numbers 32:23, NIV)

All of the signs were becoming more and more obvious. Something was going on in Ben's life that was causing him to self-destruct. As parents, we refused to believe it was drugs. Was he depressed? Did he have ADD? ADHD? OCD? Was he bi-polar? Were his testosterone levels low? Did he just need counseling? I thought, *There has to be a medical reason why this is occurring.* There is no way he would allow drug use to mess up his dream of playing college football. But things just didn't add up. Soon I had to face a reality I did not want to face, so I began investigating trying to figure it all out.

I had paid for Ben's tuition. I had paid for Ben's dorm room. I had paid for a meal plan. I had provided him a credit card to get fuel for his extravagant and overpriced jacked-up Chevy Silverado LTZ, which looked like a Cadillac on the inside. The credit card was the first area where I began exploring. There were several $25 charges on it that I could not identify. Exactly $25. No cents. All to the same store. I researched the store and learned it was what many refer to as a "head shop." If you Google this term, one of the top listings is found on urbandictionary.com, a site that gives modern day slang definitions for words or phrases that may not be found in the normal dictionary. Urban Dictionary defines a head shop as "a store that sells smoking implements and accessories for marijuana." The website is even kind enough to give you a few examples to help you understand the context and how the words might be used in a sentence. "I just picked up a fine bong from the head shop in West Ed. Shall we go burn one?" "I am going to the head shop to buy a bong." "Man that final exam was a beast, I'm gonna swing by the head shop and try and relax." The website also gives you a list of several words related to head shop: Bong, weed, marijuana, pipe, bowl, high, blunt, piece, smoke, stoner, cannabis, pothead, drugs, legal highs, pipes.

I called the head shop and asked the very laid back, smooth talking, worthless piece of garbage proprietor what in his store might a person buy for $25 total, no cents. He replied, "Ha ha, um, that would be hard to say, man." Soon, however, I got an introduction to what is known as legal marijuana or synthetic marijuana. It's often sold under the brand name Spice or K2. Each bag contains dried or shredded leaves or plant materials of some sort that have had a chemical additive applied to it. When smoked it has a psychoactive or mind-altering effect. It is labeled "not for human consumption," but that doesn't stop people from using it. For all anyone knows, some guy in the mountains took dried out plant leaves and sprayed chemicals on them with an old Windex bottle.

No one who uses this stuff has any idea what is going into their body.

This stuff was not regulated. And head shops were not the only places in Oxford, or probably near your town, where synthetic marijuana was sold. It was also sold in gas stations and over the Internet. So at that time, any 12-year-old could go into a gas station selling Spice or K2 and legally buy the product. Yes, *legally buy the product.* It was sold as incense. So there was no age limit and no ID required. *Literally* anyone could buy the product. Oh, and it did not show up on a NCAA drug test because the chemicals used changed frequently and there really was not any testing available at the time to detect it. The United States military was having a problem with this as well because our soldiers could use this stuff and they knew it would not show up on a random drug test.

After my research I told Joni what I had found out. I knew we were indeed dealing with a drug problem, but I just didn't know to what extent. It was only April, so I thought maybe if we confronted Ben and took some immediate action, then maybe he would realize that he needed to change course, study hard for final exams, put this semester behind him, and get serious about school and about life.

I mentioned the author and speaker Steve Farrar earlier. Occasionally Steve shares some stories about his son John's choices during his senior year in high school. After a few poor choices, Steve felt like he needed to get John's attention quickly while his son still lived at home. John got up one morning and was about to drive to school, but he discovered that his Jeep was not in the driveway where he had left it the night before. John said, "Dad where is my Jeep?" Steve replied, "Oh, I gave it to the family down the street. You know, the family who lately has been having a rough time financially? They needed a vehicle so I gave them the Jeep. Oh, and just to remind you, the Jeep was my Jeep, not your Jeep." As you can imagine, John was furious. "But Dad, how do you expect me to get to school?" Steve countered, "John, there's an amazing thing. Every morning at the exact same time, there is this large yellow vehicle that stops right in front of our driveway. It's called a school bus, and it drives kids to school, and it even brings them home every afternoon." John was about to come unglued and fired back, "But, Dad, I am a senior!" Steve calmly replied, "Yeah, that's great. And you know what? You will probably be the biggest kid on the bus."

After I shared my findings with Joni, she looked at me and said, "Go get his truck." She immediately knew what we should do, though she had never been to a Steve Farrar men's conference!

The last few times Ben and I were together it had been under tense circumstances. He had displayed a level of anger that frightened me. Quite honestly, I was a little scared of him. I decided to find someone to go with me to Oxford, not only to drive his truck back, but also to be there if he became angry and lashed out at me. I called Andy, a friend who was the worship pastor at my church and who lives in the adjoining neighborhood. He was outside mowing, and his wife took the phone to him outside. I had no other choice but to be blunt and honest. "Andy, is there any way you can stop what you are doing and go to Oxford with me? I have to go get Ben's truck." My voice then began to break, and I started crying as I got the next sentence out. "My boy has gotten into drugs, and I just need to go get his truck." He told me to come get him; he would be ready in two minutes.

I honestly don't recall what Andy and I talked about on the way. At some point I shared that I did not know how Ben would react, which was one reason I had called him. Did I mention that Andy can bench about 400 pounds? He makes the man of steel look like a flabby fellow in blue tights and a red speedo!

Ben's phone had a feature where you could track it if it were lost or stolen. So instead of alerting him I was on my way, I found out where his phone was and we drove straight there. He was at a friend's apartment, a friend with whom I was familiar. I knocked on the apartment door where he was, and Ben opened the door. As you can imagine, he was shocked to see me there, but I don't think he was really surprised. I told him I had come to take his truck home and sell it. I didn't ask what he had been doing. I simply reminded him that if he chose to use drugs, then I was no longer obligated to provide him with a vehicle. He did not argue the point. He simply walked out and got the things from the truck he needed and handed me the keys. Before we drove off I reminded him all of his classes were within walking distance of his dorm and he had three meals a day waiting for him in the school cafeteria. I also said I had added money to his student ID card for him to use for soft drinks and snacks, so he had everything he needed to go to class, study, eat, sleep, and finish the semester strong.

Ben later told me that when he opened the door that day his dorm roommate was standing inside with about $4,000 cash in his hands. The money came from him being able to steal and sell Xanax. I had not noticed the cash. I also did not realize Ben had begun a love affair with Xanax by this time. When he needed to concentrate and be alert, he would find Adderall or Vyvanse. He had even begun snorting it, which makes the effect immediate and intense as it goes straight to the brain. Then, when he needed to calm down, he would find Xanax.

Andy and I left Oxford with Ben's truck, which originally cost about $50,000. I did not pay that, but regardless, what a ridiculous high school graduation gift to ever give a kid! I bought the truck from a local customization shop. About once a year, the shop owner would buy a brand new top of the line truck with all the bells and whistles. He would then have tens of thousands of dollars worth of accessories added to the vehicle. He added a customized lift kit, custom rims, oversized tires, DVD player, hydraulic running boards, and several other items. This was his "show" truck when people came to his shop looking for similar customizations. I bought the two-year-old vehicle from him for $27,000. I still can't believe I got it for that price. It was basically book value on the truck without the customizations. I owned the truck for about 17 months, and Ben put about 20,000 miles on it. When I got home I listed it for sale for $28,000. I sold it within two hours sight unseen to a guy in Indiana who had it picked up the following day by an 18-wheeler. I think that may have been God's way of patting me on the shoulder and at least reaffirming that I made the right decision and was doing the right things.

But I was mad.

I was mad at Ben. I was mad that a gas station could sell synthetic marijuana to 12-year-olds. And I was mad at myself for my little by little compromises, over the previous year. As I thought of the compromises I wondered if I had contributed to any of this madness.

I could not do much about any of it, but I wanted to do something about gas stations selling drugs "legally." First, I went back to Oxford to bring Ben home at the end of the semester. I also arranged a meeting with Coach Nutt to make sure he knew of this new drug that wasn't detected on NCAA drug tests. He was shocked, and said he honestly thought I was mistaken. He shared with me that just the day prior he had been in meetings where the NCAA drug-testing representative assured him that their test was picking up everything on their list. What I explained to him, and he quickly verified, was that the synthetic substance was so new, it was not on anyone's list. He was appreciative that I met with him. He even encouraged Ben to come back to the team if he could get his life in order.

I then called Rita Martinson, my local state representative. I asked, "Rita, how does a plain ole' citizen like me get a law passed in Mississippi?" She replied, "Well, you just took the first step." I shared my findings with her, and she verified the facts with the Mississippi Bureau of Narcotics. Within a couple of weeks she had authored legislation similar to other states outlawing Spice, K2, and similar substances. The problem was, the legislature did not reconvene until January of the following year.

However, over the summer the governor called a special session about another matter, and the Spice ban was added to the special session. On August 27, the governor signed a law outlawing synthetic marijuana in Mississippi.

Now put that in your bong and smoke it, Mr. Head Shop owner!

Chapter 11

Pride Aside

Be alert and of sober mind. Your enemy the devil
prowls around like a roaring lion looking for
someone to devour. (1 PETER 5:8, NIV)

Ben failed more classes than he passed that semester. He came home for
the summer. But he said he wanted to go back to Ole Miss and make
everything right. He talked about using the university's forgiveness policy,
which allows a student to retake two classes and replace a poor grade with
a better one. He said he could take a couple of short intercession classes,
which were two week classes meeting four hours a day where a student
could complete an entire semester of class in only two weeks. This would
get his hours back to where they needed to be. Ben also said he wanted to
play football.

Again, it is so easy for me to look back and with clarity of hindsight
understand what he was thinking. Yes, of course he wanted to do all of
those things. But not for a second did he want to give up the third life
of drugs and alcohol so he could concentrate on academics and athletics.
Like most drug addicts, he just wanted to try the whole process over again
and see if he could manage it better this time.

Notice I have moved from calling Ben a young man who
experimented, to a young man who abused some drugs by taking them

the wrong way, to now referring to him as an addict. I didn't see it then, but looking back I think he clearly was an addict.

At that point, however, I never considered addiction. In my mind, I believed he was a kid for whom life was too easy. I simply thought he just needed to learn from his mistakes, create new goals, put himself in a position to accomplish those goals, then everything would be great. For many kids that age, this is what happens. For a high percentage of kids who experiment with drugs or alcohol, at some point they use too much, and they learn from that mistake and realize they can't do that anymore. Sometimes there is an accompanying negative consequence like a car wreck or an arrest. Then they come to the realization that it was not worth it, so they stop. But a small percentage of teens don't seem to learn from overuse or from negative consequences, and it is this group that probably has a true addiction.

If you research why this might be true, you will find several different "expert" opinions. You may find the medical community calling addiction a disease. You may find the psychological community calling it a symptom that looks like a disease, but is not a disease. You may find the religious community calling it a disconnect from God. But one thing you will definitely find, without question, if you research for hours and days, reading countless studies, articles, and blogs, is that no one knows for sure what addiction is, how to define it, and how to treat it. If they did, there would not be varying opinions, varying treatment options, and continual relapse. Research shows that some addicts are poor, some are rich; some are black, some are white; some are old, some are young; some are boys, some are girls; some are parents, some are grandparents; some had a great family, while others came from broken homes. No definitive conclusion can be drawn as to what causes someone to become an addict. There have been studies done on twins that claim to prove children of addicts are eight times more likely to become an addict, which means the problem is in the person's gene pool. Most studies indicate addiction can be attributed half to genetics and half to environment. In other words, a person could have heart disease partially because heart disease runs in their family and partially because they eat bacon cheeseburgers three times a day.

The only thing anyone knows for sure is that nobody knows for sure why some people become addicts and others do not!

So why do I now think Ben was an addict at this point?

Drug use had made Ben's life unmanageable. Again, I did not see it then as clearly as I see it now. But the desire to be high, which at some point became a need to get high or an actual chemical dependency, outweighed all other normal desires.

One reason people say addiction is not a disease is because the person first had to choose to use drugs. The argument is that while a person does not choose to get cancer or diabetes, at some point a person makes a decision to drink alcohol, abuse a legal drug, or take an illegal drug. So at one point in time, it was a choice. However, some people can stop using, and some people cannot. For those that cannot, I believe it does somewhat become a disease.

Consider this graph below:

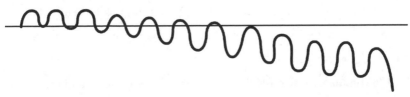

Each arch represents when a person got high. The flat line going across represents life in general or how the person feels on a normal day, if drugs or alcohol are not a part of their life. So notice the first arch--the first time the person got high. They started off the day on the flat line. Then they got high, which made the arch go up--they felt great in some way. After the drug wore off they came back down to the flat line where they had started. But notice after a few times of getting high, about one-third of the way across the chart. The top of the arch does not go as high and then it bottoms out below the line. This is because they develop a tolerance to the drug, and subsequent use does not make them as high as it once did. Then notice about two-thirds of the way across the chart, the top of the arch does not even make it up to the flat line. This means after continued use, they have to use daily just to feel normal. They have to get high just to get back up to the flat line, but eventually they cannot even get back up to the flat line. By this time they have doubled or tripled the amount they originally started using when it was first a choice. Now it is no longer a choice, however. They have to use. This is when the involuntary part of the brain kicks in and overrides the voluntary part of the brain. They literally no longer have a choice--they have to get high or they feel like they are dying. At this point, I believe they have a disease. It is no longer the person making the decisions; it is the disease making the decisions. Addicts call it being sick and getting well. They call themselves sick when they are at the bottom of an arch; they have to use just to get well.

So how is this possible?

Again, a person can go crazy reading articles and medical journals trying to figure this out. After all of my reading, I think I can make the following generalization.

Our brains are obviously very complex. I do not understand the brain. But I do know some parts of the brain deal with voluntary actions. You decided to eat breakfast this morning, you decided to watch television, or you decided to read this book. Other parts of the brain deal with involuntary actions. You continue to breathe after you fall asleep because your brain forces you to, your blood still flows through your body, or your heart still continues to beat. You are not choosing for these things to happen, your brain is choosing or forcing these things to happen for you. Initially, a person makes a conscious decision to drink alcohol, abuse a legal drug, or take an illegal drug. But brain scans performed on addicts have shown that addiction "lives" in the involuntary areas of the brain. At first it was a decision they made, but at some point for some people, the addiction begins to inhabit the involuntary area. Without some sort of treatment or intervention, the person must use, otherwise they feel as if they are going to die. They become like an alligator seeing food. An alligator does not have the part of the brain that makes voluntary decisions. An alligator only has the small involuntary part of the brain. That is why no one can train an alligator. If an alligator sees food, an alligator eats food. If he sees a puppy on the edge of the lake, he eats the puppy on the edge of the lake. An addict eventually gets to that point. He has to use in order to survive, or so he believes.

The only cure I know that works without question is to never start. Hopefully something will occur in a person's life that will keep them from ever making that choice to use drugs or alcohol for the first time.

For me, it was Len Bias.

The NBA draft, the NFL draft, and all of the professional sports drafts work the same way. Basically, if you are the worst team in the country one year, you get the top draft pick the following year and you get the best college player in the country to join your team. If you are the best team in the country one year, you get the last draft pick the following year. This way, it helps the bad teams get better, and prevents the good teams from being overly dominant. However, teams can trade and buy draft selections. A team might trade a player for a better draft selection the following year. A good team might trade a bad team one of their players, and maybe even some cash, in return for one of the bad team's good draft picks. This is the only way a good team can get a good draft selection.

This is what happened between the Boston Celtics and the Seattle Supersonics in 1984. The Celtics were the team of the 80s. They won the NBA Championship in 1981, 1984, and 1986; they also made it to the NBA finals in 1985 and 1987. In 1986 they had an incredible record of 67-15 and made basketball look easy with a starting lineup of Larry Bird, Kevin McHale, Robert Parish, Dennis Johnson, and Danny Ainge. This does not even count the fact they had Bill Walton on the bench. Bill Walton would have started and been the star on any other NBA team that year, yet he was the Celtics sixth man! On June 8, 1986, in front of a home crowd at Boston Garden, the Celtics defeated the Houston Rockets (114-97) for the NBA Championship. This should have meant they would have the last pick in the 1986 NBA draft nine days later.

Two years prior, however, on October 16, 1984, Boston traded Gerald Henderson to Seattle for some cash and a 1986 first round draft pick. So on June 17, 1986, when that draft finally rolled around, the Boston Celtics chose Len Bias from the University of Maryland. The best team just got one of the best college players in the United States. The buzz in the sporting world was how the Celtics, who had been almost unbeatable, would now be even more unbeatable. The Celtics already had a basketball dynasty. Sports writers were looking to coin new words or phrases to describe how good this team was soon-to-be.

Len Bias, however, would never wear the Celtic green and white. He would never step foot on the parquet floor of Boston Garden. Instead, he and his father would fly back to Maryland the following day for an NBA club draft acceptance and product endorsement signing ceremony. He was about to sign a five-year, multi-million dollar endorsement deal with Reebok. He drove his newly leased sports car back to his former Maryland campus and ate dinner with some former teammates. Around 2:00 a.m. on June 19 he went to a party off campus and was back in his dorm around 3:00 a.m. At some point during the next three hours he used cocaine. Many claim it was his first time; others claim it was at least one of his first few times. Regardless, after using cocaine he had a seizure and collapsed at 6:30 a.m. He was pronounced dead at 8:55 a.m. at Leland Memorial Hospital in Riverdale, Maryland of a cardiac arrhythmia related to cocaine usage.

There were no other drugs or alcohol found in his system.

I was 20 years old on that Thursday morning. I remember watching the news and thinking to myself, *I will never put anything like that inside of me. Who knows if I might be the one who dies after using one time?*

For those who do start and at some point become dependent, the process toward dependency evolves differently for all of them. But eventually there are only two outcomes to addiction: people either stop using or they die.

Ben would come close to stopping several times over the next few years. And many times he would also come close to dying.

Chapter 12

Pride  Aside

For all that is in the world, the lust of the flesh and
the lust of the eyes and the boastful pride of life, is
not from the Father, but is from the world.
(1 JOHN 2:16, NASB)

Once again, Ben struck a deal with Joni and me. Actually, he struck a few deals. First, he would go back to school for the second part of the summer session and take two accelerated classes. He would make As in those two classes, submit to the rules we set forth for the fall, and we would try again.

At that time, I was what some people refer to as a "road warrior." I didn't travel all the time, but I had traveled once or twice a month for a night or two at a time for the previous 10 years. I am one of those weirdoes who likes to see how many travel points he can accumulate. Laugh if you want, but I have two million Hilton points and can stay at a cheap Hampton Inn for 200 nights if Joni ever boots me out of the house!

So I got a room for Ben at the Hampton Inn of Oxford while he took these classes. In the meantime I helped look for a place for him to live for the upcoming fall semester. During the summer, Ben made a couple of As. He actually made a B in one of the classes, but at my insistence he emailed the professor and sweet-talked an A out of her. This made him academically eligible for football again, but he wanted to wait until the spring to return to the team. He was out of shape, had lost weight again, and knew he would not play that fall. So he thought if he got back in good shape over the fall and impressed the coaches in the spring, he would play a good bit the following fall. Sounded logical, right?

It's hard to argue with a man with a plan.

Once again, Daddy thought if he could somehow make Ben happy and put him in a good situation, he would appreciate it so much that he would try harder than ever to do well in school, do well in athletics, and have a happy life. Growing up, Ben had a good friend who was one year younger than him and who was about to become an incoming freshman at Ole Miss. They wanted to be roommates. We knew the young man very well. He grew up three doors down from us and was a good kid. He was never in any trouble, had a great mom, and also a well-rounded older brother. I helped Ben and his friend look for a house to rent off campus, and found one less than one mile away that would work out well. I signed a six-month lease, took care of all of the utilities, and the friend's mom paid his half. I got them dishes for their cabinets, silverware for their drawers, a couch, chair, coffee table, dining room table, cable TV, and wireless Internet. Everything a hard working college student needed, right? Oh, I also got them a grill for their deck and some decorative tiki torches. I mean, a guy has to grill on game day! I installed a landline telephone in Ben's room so I could call him and assure that he was awake when he was supposed to be and on his way to class before it started. I insisted he allow me to have a level of accountability so we knew he was following through with his promises. I installed a fax machine on his desk so bills and receipts could be sent back and forth. I even had him text me a picture from class to show that he was there. He did not have a regular credit card this time. He had a Shell credit card so he could get fuel, and I mailed a small amount of cash each week so he never had very much, but had enough for a few incidentals. I drove to Oxford every other week and took him to the grocery store and bought two weeks worth of food. I also placed money on his college ID that he could use at vending machines around campus for soft drinks and snacks. I helped him draft emails to his professors from the previous semester, asking how he could finish incomplete projects and better his grade. I bought him a piece of junk car to get back and forth to class--a far cry from the luxury truck he had been driving. So he had a nice place to live, reasonable transportation, accountability, very little cash, and no access to credit cards other than for fuel.

Ben's deal with us lasted a few weeks.

Before midterm exams rolled around, he had quit going to class. He never even went in to take any of his midterm exams. He called one day and said the Shell card was not working. I had just paid the bill a few days prior, so I got online to see what the issue was. In one week he put $600 worth of gas on the card, which was the credit limit. He began filling other peoples cars with gas in exchange for cash or drugs. He wiped out the $100 or so on his student ID by buying people soft drinks and chips out of the vending machines, in exchange for a dollar here and a dollar there. After that I probably spent one or two days a week driving back and forth to Oxford trying to get him to go to class, taking away any means of bartering he had, and showing him how to contact professors to try to salvage each class. If he could somehow just pass the classes then if he ever did straighten up at least he would have the ability to continue school.

Just before the end of the semester he decided to take a road trip and attend a party in Starkville, on the campus of Mississippi State University. The two campuses are just 90 miles apart, so it's not uncommon for students to go back and forth to see each other. Ben ended up being arrested that night for DUI and Minor In Possession. This was his second arrest--both of which were DUIs--and included an extra charge for good measure. As a result I also found out he had numerous speeding tickets from the Oxford police as well as the Mississippi Highway Patrol.

I think Ben ended up passing three classes and failing one that semester. To be honest, the entire fall was a blur to me. Not only was I spending crazy amounts of money trying to get him through the semester, but also I was earning less because of the hours I was not spending to maintain my own business.

The semester finally came to an end.

And while he got in a deep hole in the middle of the semester, he climbed out. Well, actually he did not; I went up there and pulled him out. He did not get out by much, and he was dirty and smelly when it happened, but the semester finally ended. He packed everything he could in his piece of junk car and came home. I drove to Oxford once again to cut off the utilities and turn the keys in to the leasing agency. He said he cleaned the house up some, but I was sure I would need to put some final touches on the house to get my security deposit back. So I took some Windex and a few other items. When I walked into the house it looked like it had been ransacked. Not only was there trash everywhere, but also there was a hole in the wall by the front door the size of a person. It actually looked like a person had been thrown into the wall, and left a hole outlining their form. There were five or six other holes in the walls, mostly fist size holes. And there was enough trash lying around to halfway fill a dumpster.

I had 28 hours before the landlord would come for inspection. It was my name on the lease, not Ben's. I had to get that place ready. I called a carpet cleaning company and scheduled a cleaning for 11:00 a.m. the following morning, one hour before inspection. So I had 27 hours to perform a miracle. I took some of the broken wall to the paint store, matched the paint, bought painting supplies, a couple of sheets of drywall, sheetrock tape and mud, and got started working 27 straight hours through the night. When the landlord arrived, he thought the place looked better than when he rented it to us.

Though Oxford is a beautiful town and Ole Miss is an elegant campus, I drove away from there with a misplaced hatred and disdain, hoping I would never have to step foot in that town again.

Chapter 13

Pride  Aside

Still, if you set your heart on God and reach out to
him, if you scrub your hands of sin and refuse to
entertain evil in your home, you'll be able to face
the world unashamed and keep a firm grip on life,
guiltless and fearless. (JOB 11:13-15, MSG)

By now you may be thinking to yourself, *OK, it's time to cut this kid loose*
and let him experience some harsh consequences. Or maybe you think, *Ben*
just needs help; serious help. But keep in mind--at this point we truly did
not grasp the full scope of what was going on. We suspected, but did not
know. We never found a big bag of drugs. He had not been arrested for
drugs. Whenever he had a setback he would always do a little better for a
while. Yes, there were signals, but as a parent you want to think the least
negative thoughts, not the *most* negative thoughts. We knew there were
drug-related things happening, but we had no idea at that point how
much he was using or the type of drugs he was using. We had no idea
the DEA had been in touch with Ben because his name had come up in
several conversations and investigations around Oxford.

So there we were at Christmas break, with Ben at home. We entered
a new phase of our relationship. As much as we loved Ben, wanted to be
with Ben, wanted to help and guide him through his struggles, we also

no longer wanted him in our house. He was angry all of the time. By this time there were several holes in the walls of our home where he had gotten angry about something and hit a wall. One time he got angry and punched the glass door of the double oven in the kitchen, which shattered into a million pieces.

Ben was a sponge.

He did nothing to earn money, yet he needed money. He slept all day and stayed up all night. He no longer wanted to be in our house either. It was just horrible. Joni and I could not sleep wondering what he was doing. I could not work because I spent half my days either trying to get him out of bed or checking on him. We did not want him in our house, but what could we do? Kick him out? That's probably what we should have done, but it's not even something we considered. After all, he was 19 years old. We thought he just needed to snap out of it and get college under his belt so he could have a happy life, right?

Soon we had another discussion. Ben said he wanted to go take two classes again, make As like he did during the last Intersession class schedule, and start football again in the spring. Of course we did not think this would work, but we wanted him out of our house. So he went back to the Hampton Inn for two weeks in Oxford and took two classes.

On the morning he was supposed to take his two finals, I got a text message saying, "I screwed up bad this time, school and football are over for me, and none of it can be fixed."

Instead of studying the night before his finals, he went out and got drunk and high. He beat up some guy at a bar and was then chased by police on foot and found hiding behind a dumpster. He had marijuana in his jacket pocket, but of course he said it was someone else's. He was charged with possession of marijuana, public drunkenness, disturbing the peace, and resisting/evading arrest.

He came home.

But we didn't want him here and he didn't want to be here either. Going back to school was obviously not an option at that point. We would have to be tough. We had to get some kind of handle on this. We had to figure out a way to get to the root of what was going on. So we decided he could stay in our house if he worked and went to counseling. He did a few odd jobs, but he literally would not get out of bed until three in the afternoon. There would be fits of rage and then times of calm and happiness. We set him up with a counselor who specialized in "delayed adolescence." The counselor worked with young people who just could not move forward in life in a positive way. Joni and I had to drive him to his appointments because his license was suspended for 90 days from his second DUI.

I had to take a business trip to Charlotte, North Carolina in late February, and it was there I got a call from Ben.

"Mom is freaked out. We are in her car, she can't breathe, I don't know what to do." I could hear Joni in the background gasping for breath and trying to speak and cry and yell but nothing was making sense. I told Ben to call 911. I then called our younger son Michael, who was 16 years old at the time. He witnessed most of what was going on with Ben but did not understand any of it either. I told Michael to get home, that I had no idea what was going on, but told him to find out and then call me.

What had happened was that Joni was driving Ben to his counseling appointment after spending hours trying to get him out of bed. As they were driving Ben became belligerent saying he did not want to go to counseling any longer, that this whole process was stupid and the guy was an idiot. Joni did the right thing and told him this was his only option right now. Otherwise he could pack his stuff and get out. Ben became enraged and started hitting the dash of the Lexus and the windows. Then, he lifted his feet and literally began kicking the windshield, shattering it into a million pieces and making it almost impossible to see through. Joni does not really remember how they got home. Her mind shut her body down. The only thing she remembers is she didn't want the 911-response team to find them. She did not know what would happen if the police or paramedics arrived, so she somehow got the car home so they would not be found.

There I was in North Carolina.

There were no more flights I could find to get me home that night. I was scheduled on the first flight out the following day. But I knew I had to get Ben away from the house. I called him and told him to pack some stuff and just get out and start walking. And he did…for about 10 minutes. Then he went back home. He sat down with his mom and said, "I know what the problem is. I have been doing more drugs than you guys know about." She discovered the reason he slept all day was because he would climb out of the second story window of his bedroom and get high all night while sitting on the roof, then he would sleep throughout the day. His counselor knew about all of this. When Ben first met his counselor he said, "Before I say a word, I have a question. Can you tell my parents anything I tell you?" The counselor said "No." Then Ben said, "My problem is drugs." So Ben was trying to stop using on his own and his counselor was trying to hold him accountable. The reason he did not want to go to his appointment that day was because he had been high for several days and knew his counselor would know.

Ben agreed to go to treatment.

The one thing I have always heard is that if someone agrees to go to treatment, you take the person right then. I called his counselor from North Carolina and he made a quick call to a rehab facility in south Mississippi. Within two hours Joni and Ben were pulling into the parking lot of what we will call Treatment Center #1. Joni had driven in a major rainstorm all the while trying to see through the spider web of cracks in the windshield. Joni left Ben with the treatment team so they could perform their intake assessment, and she drove back to Madison hoping to get a few hours of sleep before going to work at 6:30 a.m.

Upon assessing Ben, it was determined he needed to go to the hospital for detox, and afterward could come back to begin treatment. So that night they transported him by ambulance to South Central Regional Medical Center in Laurel, Mississippi. The next day in the hospital, he met BB and Mike who were also there for detox. Mike was in really bad shape and having a horrible time. He was shaking and sweating. Ben and BB came up with a solution that is typical of most addicts. They decided to get Mike some drugs so he would not be so uncomfortable. So that night BB climbed through a ceiling tile of a room they could access. He inched his way over the hall hoping to climb down into the locked pharmacy area and retrieve a few items for Mike…and also for he and Ben while he was there. Ben sat in the hall to keep an eye out for the hospital staff. One of the staff members approached Ben and quizzed him about why he was in the hall. About that time, BB fell through the roof of the pharmacy. So BB was arrested.

My phone rang once again at 2:00 a.m.

It was a hospital staff member telling me of BB's arrest. I also learned they had kicked Ben out of the hospital and threatened to press charges against him the following day. Ben had begun walking away from the property in another driving rainstorm. A security guard was nice enough to catch him and put him on the phone. I have worked in Laurel before, and I knew there was a Hampton Inn across the street from the hospital. I told Ben to go there, that I would have a room waiting on him, and I would be there in a few hours. Ben was asleep in the room when I arrived.

I spent the morning doing damage control. I had a good friend who was an OB/GYN and delivered most of the babies at that hospital. He called the hospital administration to smooth things over and let them know Ben was going to treatment. They agreed not to pursue any charges. I then called the treatment center and informed them of all that had happened. They were unaware of any of the hospital incident. They asked if Ben had used any drugs after being kicked out of the hospital, which might require him to continue detox, and fortunately he had not.

But he had tried.

Instead of going straight to the Hampton Inn like I had asked, Ben walked in the rain pulling his little suitcase to a gas station and then to a Waffle House, trying to find someone with drugs. Luckily he failed, and made it to the Hampton Inn around 3:30 a.m., just a few minutes before my arrival. The treatment center agreed to have Ben come back at 3:00 that afternoon.

There was a one-week blackout period at Treatment Center #1 where the clients are not allowed to make or receive calls. That was a good week for us. As devastated, humiliated, scared, and embarrassed as we were with the whole situation, we knew he was safe. Treatment centers are not jails. Clients can leave whenever they want, unless they have been court ordered. Even then they can still leave, they just may face legal consequences later. But as long as we did not get a call saying that he had left treatment, we knew he was safe, warm, well fed, and hopefully seeking answers. Over the next few years we really only rested and slept well when Ben was in treatment.

One of the first calls I got from Ben was mid-morning the following week. He had stormed out of a group counseling session and picked up the phone in the hallway. "Come get me out of this (Bad Word) place. Everyone here is a (Bad Word) idiot. They don't know a (Bad Word) thing about any of this (Bad Word)." I could hear one of the staff saying, "Ben, you need to hang up the phone and come back to the session." Ben told them, "I am talking to my dad right now, this is all a bunch of (Bad Word)." They calmly said, "Ben, you need to hang up the phone and come back to the session, right now." He told them, "I am out of here, and my dad is going to come get me." They reiterated, "Ben, hang the phone up, now." Ben then said to me in a defeated voice, "I have to go." And then he hung up. I have to be honest, Joni and I laughed pretty hard as I shared the story with her. Although it was not funny, all we knew to do was to laugh. But it was really a very telling phone call. Ben's first reaction to apparently being confronted in the group session by a very qualified counselor was to "go call Daddy." The counselor apparently pointed out some things to Ben about his need to take responsibility for his actions and to stop coming up with excuses and blaming circumstances.

Ben did not want to look at himself through that type of microscope, so he decided to make a call and hope Daddy would fix it.

I would learn more and more about this whole addiction thing over the next few years and the next few rehabs. I would learn more about terms like enabling and co-dependency. To this day, I still struggle with the proper balance of what is actually helping versus hurting Ben. For me, and I assume for most parents, I found myself thinking if I could keep him from making a huge mistake, at some point he would snap out of it and get better. Then, he would not have a felony conviction or a bankruptcy on his record. As a parent I got to a point where I was OK with small consequences being levied against him, but I just did not want any big ones. And at the same time, I just wanted him well.

But I was not helping him get well by constantly bailing him out when he had trouble in school, had speeding tickets that needed to be paid, or needed things smoothed over with people so more charges would not be filed. I was only teaching him he did not have to take responsibility; I would take it for him. I was starting to understand this. But still I was adamant if I could keep something really bad from happening, one day he could move on with a clean slate. I think I was just as sick as he was, only in a different way.

We visited Ben on Saturdays.

Ben watched an older client fall over and die, succumbing to years of alcohol abuse. We attended family sessions and began to learn some of the terms we would use over the next few years, as well as some of the psychology and pharmacology behind addiction. We learned Ben would be encouraged to go to AA meetings the rest of his life. Really? He was just 20 years old. I don't think there is a 20 year old on earth who, upon learning he needs to be in AA forever, thinks to himself *That's something I plan to do for the rest of my life.* This is because 20-year-olds are bulletproof. They do not have a concept of life-long anything. At least I did not think Ben did. We also learned that other families were hurting just as much as we were. We were not alone. And other families had been through this multiple times. We heard that other families had found their son or daughter passed out with a needle in their arm. I remember thinking, *Thank goodness we caught this now so we will not have to go through any of that.*

But I was wrong.

Chapter 14

Pride  Aside

These commandments that I give you today are to be upon your hearts. Impress them on your children. Talk about them when you sit at home and when you walk along the road, when you lie down and when you get up. Tie them as symbols on your hands and bind them on your foreheads. Write them on the doorframes of your houses and on your gates. (DEUTERONOMY 6:6-9, NIV)

Ben came home after spending a month at Treatment Center #1 and did great. He got up every morning and he made his bed.

Not long ago Joni told me that U.S Navy Admiral William H. McRaven was asked to deliver the commencement address at the University of Texas – Austin, where he had graduated 37 years prior. McRaven acknowledged and agreed with the premise of the university slogan, "What starts here changes the world." I watched the video of his address in which he gave 10 key points that graduates could use for the rest of their lives to change the world. When anyone comes up with a list of 10 key points, they usually put the main point first. If a person can take this first main point and implement it into their lives, then McRaven argued they could change the world. So what was his first main point?

I was sitting on the edge of my chair waiting to hear from this 36-year Navy Seal, who was head of U.S. Special Operations Command and recipient of the Defense Distinguished Service Medal, Defense Superior Service Medal, Legion of Merit, and two Bronze Stars.

McRaven said, first and foremost, if you want to change the world, "Make your bed."

Huh?

He explained, "Every morning, in Seal training, my instructors, who at the time were all Vietnam veterans, would show up in my barracks room, and the first thing they would do was inspect my bed. If you did it right, the corners would be square, the covers would be pulled tight, the pillow centered just under the headboard, and the extra blanket folded neatly at the foot of the rack. It was a simple task, mundane at best, but every morning we were required to make our bed to perfection. That seemed a little ridiculous at the time, particularly in light of the fact that we were aspiring to be real warriors, tough, battle-hardened Seals. But the wisdom of this simple act has been proven to me many times over.

If you make your bed every morning you will have accomplished the first task of the day. It will give you a small sense of pride, and it will encourage you to do another task, and another, and another. And by the end of the day, that one task completed will have turned into many tasks completed. Making your bed will also reinforce the fact that the little things in life matter. If you can't do the little things right, you will never be able to do the big things right. And if by chance you have a miserable day, you will come home to a bed that is made. That you made. And a made bed gives you encouragement that tomorrow will be better. So if you want to change the world, start off by making your bed."

We never required Ben to make his bed growing up. At that time it seemed like regularly I was bombarded with little bits of information or advice that made me feel like a total failure as a parent. I constantly looked back and analyzed everything. Should I have done this? Why did I not do that? If only we had required Ben to make his bed, none of this would have happened. Not only was I trying to do the things necessary from this point forward to help Ben get well, but I was also beating myself up daily about what I could have done differently in the past that might have prevented his spiral altogether.

About the same time Joni shared this bed-making information, I was also working on a project for Baptist Health Systems and the Mississippi Baptist Convention. It was the development of a six-week DVD-led Bible study. The project was designed to give churches and individuals a tool to help people be healthier both physically and spiritually. A panel of four physicians was tapped to film six thirty-minute sessions in which they gave practical, medical advice covering topics like general health, cancer, diabetes, heart health, and intimacy. When the topic of obesity came around, Dr. Bill Harper shared more than just some practical medical advice. Dr. Harper, a cardiologist, is a native Mississippian and a graduate of Ole Miss and the University of Mississippi School of Medicine. Practicing since 1980, he is a Diplomate of the American Board of Internal Medicine and its subspecialty of Cardiovascular Diseases. He is a Fellow of the American College of Cardiology, and a member of the Mississippi State Medical Association. But more importantly, he is a father--and in my eyes, a good father.

In talking about obesity, Dr. Harper started out with sage practical advice.

"The world right now, especially in our country, is well aware of the issue of drinking and driving. If we talk about alcohol intake then resulting in traffic accidents, everybody is now a convert. Everybody understands that. We all now have designated drivers when there is a social outing. It's a given; you understand it; you accept it. This issue of nutrition needs to be the same; it explodes into so many aspects of healthcare.

I tell my patients let's look at your meals, tell me how you eat. They say, 'I skip breakfast. I don't hardly eat lunch,' and then they stop talking. They stop talking because they have it completely backwards. The most important meal of the day if you are trying to lose weight is breakfast."

He continued to explain the benefits of a good breakfast, a healthy lunch, and a light dinner from a medical standpoint.

But then he took a turn.

"There are patterns here that we have got to change, and they are so easy to change. And besides that, they are going to give you a healthier family. That time with your children in the morning, let me tell you, they need you to tell them something positive. The dad I hope is leading the devotional anyway, just a minute or two, read from a Proverb or what have you, but that morning hour is a time that you reassure them that they are OK and that they are loved. You know, if your children have come home with a negative comment from someone the day before like 'your ears are big' or 'your eyes are too narrow' or 'your nose is too big.' James Dobson tells us 'Do you know how many positive inputs that child or your wife has to have or your husband has to have to recover psychologically from one negative input? It takes twelve. It takes twelve positive inputs to overcome what was told to them at school yesterday.' Your opportunity to do this is in the morning. Their minds are fresh, they are listening, and you can have that little time together with them. It's just like filling up their tank with love and reassurance, whether it be your spouse or your children. Everybody needs it. They need those strokes. And then we go out into the world."

We were lucky to get a Pop-Tart into our boys' mouths in the car on the way to school most mornings. So there I was again, hearing an off the cuff story from a doctor about eating a good breakfast. At face value it is great information, but even so it left me feeling like a failure as a father. I kept thinking, *Why did we not prioritize breakfast? If only we had made breakfast a priority, our son would not be a drug addict.* That thought is silly, I know. But it seemed like every story I heard, even if it was completely unrelated, made me feel like a failure as a father.

A few moments later Dr. Harper nailed me again, unknowingly of course. Nobody ever was trying to make me feel like a failure. I mean good grief; he was talking about eating a healthy breakfast! But it seemed like I was a human decoder machine, but I was decoding his words improperly. Data would come in, it would obviously mean one thing, but I would decode the data to mean something else. It did not matter what I heard, I would translate it into how I had failed as a father.

Dr. Harper added, "A survey was done where they interviewed National Merit Finalists in this country. They looked for a common denominator. What was the most important common denominator that led them to become a National Merit Finalist? It was not whether or not the parent's had college degrees; it was not their economic level of family income; it was not their particular religious affiliation. The most important factor, the most common denominator in National Merit Finalists, was one family meal a day."

He continued, "Now I recently wrote an article and forgot about it. It was published in one of those Baptist journals, and a physician came up to me in the hospital and said, 'You have changed my life.' It was basically a little tidbit that I did on that very subject, the importance of a family meal every day. If the National Merit Finalists are at a table having a meal every day, the obvious question is, 'Are we also having that family meal?'

I told my wife before I went into private practice and came out of the military, here is the deal: if we can't have one family meal a day, I will quit private practice. I will go to the VA or back to the Army or to the University, but we are going to have a family meal every day. It is the start, it is the beginning of correcting all of those issues that follow the rest of the day, and possibly affect your children as well."

Yes, you guessed it, we did not do that either.

Every day had its scheduling challenges. Football practice for both boys, track meets for both boys, basketball games for Michael, ROTC for Michael, some travel days for me, Joni grading papers. Could we have? Of course we could have. But we did not make it a priority. So there I was feeling like a failure yet again, just because I heard a great story but translated it improperly.

Regardless of my translation issues, Ben came home from Treatment Center #1. He made his bed. He did better. He ate better. He looked better. He was nicer. He went to court in Oxford to face his four charges and took his certificate of completion from Treatment Center #1 along with him to show them he was trying to turn things around. I hired an attorney in Oxford who knew the police officers and knew the judge. Again, I felt like if Ben could turn things around and not have four convictions on his record, he could move forward in life. So I made some calls, did some research, and handpicked the attorney who had the best connections in Oxford. Sure enough, the two worst charges were dropped completely, and the other two charges would be expunged after one year, assuming he did not get in trouble in Oxford during that time.

Daddy did it again.

The summer was drawing to a close. Ben worked for a friend of his who owned a lawn cutting and landscaping service. He also spent a month in Florida. He and a couple of other guys got jobs putting out umbrellas at a resort, which paid really well. He soon found out the reason it paid so well is because it was grueling work and they could not keep anybody more than a couple of weeks. Well, he did not even last that long. Actually, the work proved to be a little too much for all of the guys that Ben was with. One of Ben's friends was so out of shape and got so overheated that he started throwing up and shaking and they had to roll him into the ocean like a beached whale to cool him off. We laugh about that now, but these guys were not in any kind of shape to be doing that kind of work.

With his umbrella-fetching career behind him, he began waiting tables. But the money he earned was not enough to pay rent, buy fuel, eat, and party the way he wanted to. He was back home in four or five weeks. We needed a plan for the fall. If college was going to be part of that plan for the fall, it was not going to be considered unless there was a goal, an objective, and a compelling reason for going back.

We talked to Ben a great deal over the summer about what he wanted to do. He had no idea what he wanted to do; he really did not. One day he wanted to own his own business, the next day he wanted to be in the FBI. Coaching football was discussed, which then morphed into becoming a Physical Therapist. PTs made good money, and they did not have to complete near as much school as medical doctors. Mississippi State University in Starkville offered several degree programs that would be a good undergraduate start for getting into PT school. So it was settled. Ben would complete the Mississippi trifecta: USM, Ole Miss, and MSU.

Go Dawgs. My closet was still full of Black and Gold from when he was at USM, and also Red and Blue from when he was at Ole Miss. But I was not about to buy anything Maroon until I saw he was progressing and doing well in school.

Although he was doing better in general, he was not following through with anything he learned in treatment. He was not going to any AA meetings and he was not working with a sponsor. He was driving again, having fulfilled all the of the court's requirements from his second DUI the previous fall. We could tell over the summer he was running and searching, trying to find happiness, and always moving to another project or even another town during the search.

I was driving back from a church in Charlotte, North Carolina where I had just hosted a Steve Farrar men's conference. I saw a call coming in on my cell phone from a number I did not recognize. I had stopped answering calls from numbers I did not recognize because some of them were bill collectors. I had never received a call from a bill collector my entire life until that time. While the important things like our mortgage and utility bills were up to date, there were a few medical bills I had let lapse hoping for insurance to kick in. We were not broke, but Ben's adventures had definitely taken a significant toll at this point on our family's finances. Whoever it was calling left a voicemail, and I listened to the voicemail.

It was Candace's mom.

Candace was a young lady friend of Ben's who graduated from the same high school. She was a party girl, but not to the extent of Ben or others she hung out with. She was always dating a "bad boy," and always seemed to be surrounded with bad boys. Ben was by then a bad boy. Jeremy, who I talked about earlier when we saw indications of Ben trying some cold medicines, was a bad boy too, and Candace loved being around him also. I hate to say this about someone's sweet daughter, but she had about as much sense as a turnip. Ben considered her one of his best friends. Regardless of how much trouble he got into or how unraveled his life was at the time, she would always be there. She would tell him everything was going to be fine, and not to worry about it. Many of Ben's other friends were already starting to distance themselves from him because they were put off by his self-destruction. But not Candace. It was like she was drawn to his self-destruction.

The voicemail from Candace's mom said Ben had taken Candace to the Mississippi Gulf Coast. Then, Ben had gotten into a fight with a guy and ended up in jail, which left Candace stranded on the gulf coast. I called the mom back and said I hated to hear about what happened. The mom asked what I planned to do about it. I said I planned to go home, eat a good dinner, and enjoy sleeping in my own bed that night. If Candace was dumb enough to go to the coast with Ben, maybe she could suddenly become smart enough to figure out how to get home on her own.

The mom hung up.

Eventually we discovered that Ben was indeed in a fight and the police were called. Ben and Candace were at Candace's "bad boy" boyfriend's house on the coast, which he shared with a roommate. Ben was high or drunk or both and was irritating the boyfriend's roommate. So, they fought. The roommate wanted Ben arrested for trespassing, but Ben was not trespassing since he was at the house as a guest of Candace's boyfriend. The police suggested Ben leave and get a hotel room, just to diffuse the situation. The police were nice enough to drive him to a hotel in hopes of eliminating more problems. The police left Ben at the hotel but the hotel manager refused to give Ben a room since he was only 20 years old. The manager then called the police again to get Ben off the hotel property. At that point the police were in a pickle. They had first tried to do a nice thing by driving Ben to a hotel, but later they did not know what to do with him.

So they arrested him for public drunkenness.

I knew Ben screwed up again. I knew he deserved to be in some sort of trouble. But my actions were driven by my logic. Ben was not drunk in public when the police originally found him. Instead, he was drunk on private property where he was an invited guest, which is not a crime. He did not become a public drunk until the officers took him off the private property. Long story short, I made a call to a friend, he made a call to friend, and the charges were dropped.

Daddy did it again.

Quite honestly, this twisted cycle was more about doing whatever I could to keep him out of trouble so he could go anywhere other than my house. The logic had shifted from trying to help Ben to trying to help me. In the family group session at Treatment Center #1, I remember the counselors talking about healthy boundaries, creating some distance, and not helping get the client out of trouble.

But what about me?

If Ben was in trouble, it caused grief and pain in my life. What about keeping him out of trouble so I could sleep better, not just so he could sleep better? What about the weight his issues put on the parents' marriage? I believed the smoother we could make his life, the smoother we could make our life. Two years earlier, parents were using Ben as an example of a positive role model to their young boys in our community. I had some parents of high school underclassmen who would call me and ask if Ben could speak to their son because their son looked up to him. Now parents were likely using Ben as an example of what not to become. They probably didn't mean to do so, but it still left a toll on Joni and me. I just needed him to be gone, out of our house, and away from us.

So off to Mississippi State he went.

Once again, we set him up in a position to win. He still had a junky car, but we signed an apartment lease at a nice complex where four boys each had a private bedroom. Each bedroom had locks that were keyed differently, but everyone shared a common area consisting of a den and a kitchen. Probably over 1,000 students lived at this complex right on the edge of campus. We again fixed his room up and got him all of his supplies and books. And once again he started the semester off great, not missing a class, and getting back on track.

Ben came home in October, but he looked horrible. He probably weighed 125-130 pounds. He was pale and had not had a hair cut in a long time. But boy was he happy. Just as happy as could be. He even had a new friend! Actually he had two new friends. Remember, new friends are a red flag. The first new friend was a guy at MSU whom he seemed to be spending all of his spare time with. He was also a high school football star who washed out in college. The other friend was a younger girl, a friend of Candace's, who also appeared to be attracted to the "bad-boy" type. But boy was Ben happy. We assumed he was happy because he was loaded the whole time he was home.

Ben spent most of his time home over at Jeremy's house. Jeremy's house, as near as we could tell, was just a free for all. The parents had no rules, and both parents used various drugs for varying medical ailments.

Users seemed to congregate there. Whenever we asked Ben who all was there, it was a Who's Who of the bad-boy community. It was always a bunch of guys who had been in trouble with the law or had problems with drugs. Ben, of course, always insisted that none of that was going on. Ben explained that he and Jeremy were just talking about things they want to do with their lives.

Then one night I got a 2:00 a.m. call.

It was Ben. He was at a gas station yelling and screaming about how he had been beaten up, and he needs a gun so he could go kill Jeremy. I got in my car and raced to the gas station, keeping him on the phone as much as I could to keep him calm until I got there. I removed the .40 Glock handgun I kept in the center console of my Yukon, removed the magazine and the round from the chamber, and then locked the gun and the ammunition in two separate compartments.

Ben got in my car wearing only a pair of blue jeans. He had no shirt, no shoes, and no socks. His face was beaten and bleeding. He acted completely insane. He was screaming that he got jumped, and that Jeremy got a gun and fired it at him trying to get him to leave. He was cussing and screaming and beating the dash of my Yukon. I begged him and begged him to stop so he would not damage my car. He would stop for a few moments and then start again. He would cuss more and beg me to let him borrow my gun so he could go shoot Jeremy. He said he just wanted to shoot him in the leg. Then a few seconds later, he said he wanted to shoot him in the face and kill him. Then he calmed down. Then it started all over again. But then he just wanted to shoot him in the leg again.

In the five to ten minutes this was going on, I was driving and trying to figure out where to take him. We could not go to a hotel because he was completely out of control. Eventually he recognized the landscape and realized I was driving him to our deer camp where we have a two-bedroom trailer. I figured nobody would be there this time of year. I thought if I got him there he would be 45 minutes away from Madison. If he did walk back in hopes of killing Jeremy, he would surely sober up before he made it all the way. When he realized we were heading to deer camp and not to Jeremy's so he could shoot him, he became enraged again. Then he punched my windshield and shattered it just like he did Joni's vehicle nine months before. He then said he was going to jump out of the car so he could go kill Jeremy.

I kept driving the 55 mph speed limit north on Highway 51 away from Madison. He opened the door and threatened to jump. I kept driving. He slammed the door and went into a rage again. I kept driving. He then opened the door again and climbed out of the car. He was standing on the running board and holding the luggage rack on the roof. Then he closed the door. I slowed to about 45 mph, but kept a steady pace, trying to find a speed fast enough that would prevent him from jumping but also slow enough that hopefully he would not be killed if he did jump. After a few miles, Ben eventually opened the door and got back in the car. He beat on the car, then stopped and cried; then beat on the car, then stopped and cried. As he cried, I reached over and rubbed his shoulders and told him how much I love him. Then I said if he really wanted to kill Jeremy when he woke up then it would be fine with me. But first, we needed to get some sleep, and then we could discuss it in the morning. Obviously, I had no intention of letting him kill Jeremy. I was just saying anything, hoping I could settle him down.

Thankfully there were no other cars at deer camp.

We went inside, turned on the AC, and looked in the fridge for anything to eat or drink that had not expired from our last trip. I joined this camp for Ben and Michael. I never hunted growing up, but all of the boys' friends did, so Ben and Michael wanted to as well. My friend David and I went in halves on a two-bedroom trailer with a kitchen, living room, and two bathrooms. We purchased three beds for the bedroom where Ben, Michael, and I slept. We also purchased three beds for the room where David and his two son's slept. We had couches, recliners, satellite television, and a nice big porch with a nice big grill. It was my dream to spend a few weekends at camp with my boys every year, but it never really worked out that way. Michael and I went quite a bit, but Ben did not really want to be there. At least he did not want to be there only with me.

Ben was in a great deal of pain from being beaten and was still raging. He asked if we had any Tylenol, but instead I gave him some allergy pills hoping they would make him drowsy so he would go to sleep. He finally did.

The next afternoon when he finally woke up, he called Jeremy and apologized. Apparently Ben was the one who started the whole altercation to begin with, and they beat him trying to get him to settle down. His phone had been shattered that night, so I took him to the Apple Store and got him a new phone and sent him back to Starkville. Once again, instead of getting in trouble, he got a new phone. And, once again, I was doing anything I could just to get him away from us.

When I got home after sending Ben back to Starkville, I found my bride of 25 years sitting in the middle of our bathroom floor. She had pulled out the six drawers in which we store our thousands of family photos. These drawers of photos contained everything from when we first met, to our wedding day, all the way through both of our boy's lives and accomplishments, up until recent days. She was sitting in the bathroom floor surrounded by thousands of photos. She slowly made her way through each drawer pulling out pictures of Ben signifying different benchmarks in his life: birth, eating his first bites of solid food, taking his first steps, pushing a toy lawnmower behind his daddy, his first day of school, his first T-ball game, all the way up to college football. Then I noticed she had a manila envelope sitting in her lap with two handwritten words penned by a black sharpie that simply said, "Ben's Funeral."

With tears rolling down her face, my wife was trying to pick out pictures for what we both thought was an imminent probability while she still had the presence of mind to do so.

Chapter 15

Pride  Aside

Finally, dear brothers and sisters, we ask you to
pray for us. Pray that the Lord's message will spread
rapidly and be honored wherever it goes, just as
when it came to you. (2 Thessalonians 3:1, NLT)

Just a few days after Ben returned to Starkville, my phone rang at 2:00 a.m.

What is it about 2:00 a.m.?

It was Josh, one of Ben's friends in Starkville. He said Ben had sent a couple of odd text messages about being sorry for everything, and that he loved him, and wished him the best in the future. Being worried, Josh went to Ben's apartment and Ben would not answer the door. He kicked Ben's door down and found that Ben was very high, coherent but obviously high, and that he had cut himself on his left upper arm in several places. None of the 15 or so wounds were serious; maybe he was just testing the waters to see what it felt like before cutting himself more severely, maybe permanently.

Josh did not know what to do. He said Ben refused to go to a hospital and was being combative. Ben kept saying he wanted to go to a party at Ole Miss, which was 90 miles away. The party was the only bargaining chip Josh had. Josh convinced Ben to go to the hospital in Oxford just to see if he needed stitches, and then they would go to the party together. They pulled out of Starkville, and I got in my Yukon and pulled out of Madison at the same time. Both of us were headed to the Oxford hospital where Ben had been to before. Their drive would take 1 hour and 45 minutes and mine would take about 2 hours and 15 minutes, but I had no intention of letting them arrive before me.

I took a chance and drove between 90 and 100 miles per hour. Fortunately I never saw a State Trooper. While I was driving, I called the emergency room in Oxford and told them that Ben was on his way, that he had tried to hurt himself, and that I felt like he was a danger to himself and others. I told them about his fits of rage, and suggested they have the police in the emergency room to protect their staff if it came to that. I also said if they were able to somehow get him sedated and place a psychiatric hold on him, I would follow through with the courts and have him committed back to treatment.

We all got to the hospital at the same time. I parked far enough away that Ben did not know I was there, but close enough that I could see and hear what was going on in the other parking lot. Ben was leery of being taken to the hospital. Josh had called a couple of friends to meet them at the hospital in case it got out of control. Ben did not want to go inside. The ER nurse I spoke to went outside and pretended to be on a smoke break. You have to love an ER nurse who takes a smoke break.

She hollered at Ben from across the parking lot in a language he could understand. She yelled, "What's the matter tough guy, scared to come into the ER? I can see your arm is bleeding from here. Want me to come out there and look at your arm since you are too big of a wus to come inside?" She walked over to Ben and looked at his arm, pointed to the worst cut, and said, "Well, that one needs stitches. If you can man up and come inside for a few minutes, we can stitch that up and send you on your way." So Ben went with her inside to the ER. He walked like a pimp from a bad 1970s movie, trying to act as tough as he could. Once inside, they gave him a shot of something that knocked him out cold. Then they placed a guard in his room and began to run tests.

I went into the ER after that, thanked Josh and the other boys for helping out, and tried to speak a small tidbit of wisdom to them about not following the same path Ben had taken. I filled out the paperwork and sat in the same waiting room I had sat in the other times he had been there for various reasons. Around daybreak, the doctor met with me and said Ben had been moved to ICU. Apparently there were indications that his kidneys were shutting down, his pancreas was doing something wrong, and his body was not responding well. I went back to see him while he was unconscious in the ICU. Ben's nurse was the older sister of one of his high school friends, and she remembered Ben's high school football days. She asked me, "Is that the Ben Hutton from MRA?" She then gave me some papers to look over and sign that wanted to verify he was an organ donor, and whether or not to resuscitate him if he died. All I could think about was the manila envelope Joni had filled with pictures just a few days earlier.

I called Joni and kept her updated.

She begged me to let her come to Oxford. My parents were visiting our home, so I begged her to stay there and just let me keep her updated for a while. But this was her son lying in ICU. Almost two hours away, her firstborn was struggling to survive. She honored my request, but retreated to the privacy of our bedroom and began to pray to our Heavenly Father. Joni and I both believe in the power of prayer, and we also both believe in the power of LOTS of prayer. We needed our friends to pray alongside us. We needed to forget about the stigma associated with drug abuse and addiction, and we needed an army of people praying for us, for Michael, and for Ben.

Joni is not the most technologically savvy person I know. But I must admit that in the few short months since I had gotten her an iPhone, she had become a texting, FaceBooking, and Pinteresting expert. And on that particular night, she was about to unleash a tech-savvy barrage against Satan and his minions who apparently were trying to steal our child. Joni was well familiar with Proverbs 16:18 (NIV) which states, "Pride comes before destruction, a haughty spirit before a fall." Joni and I were not about to let our pride bring destruction to our child. We needed prayer, we needed our friends to pray, and we needed an army of their friends to pray.

Joni simply sent out a group text to a handful of individuals in our Sunday School class that simply said, *"Pride Aside…we need prayer."*

Our Sunday School class (we call it a Life Group because all of the hip Baptist churches have renamed many of the traditional, churchy titles) became an instant source of refuge and strength. I joke about our Sunday School class now being called a Life Group, but in all honesty, it IS a more accurate description, especially for our group. Our Life Group truly did life together, throughout Ben's ongoing problems as well as during another couple's tragedy when they lost their son in a car accident that same month. As a class, we temporarily threw the church's curriculum out the window. Instead we spent every Sunday talking about what the Scriptures had been teaching each of us that week about pride, suffering, pain, guilt, hope, mercy, love, forgiveness, and more. Each week we cried together, prayed together, and shared our lives together. Our Life Group saved our lives, and continues to do so to this day. In the last chapter I will say more about the *Pride Aside* text message as well as more about our Life Group.

But at that point, Ben was still in the ICU.

His nurse apparently was just as text savvy as Joni, because she had texted her sister who was in Ben's graduating class and told her about his condition. That may have broken a few dozen HIPAA laws, but we didn't care. Ben's phone started lighting up with text messages from the sister and others with well wishes and hopes of pulling through.

As the morning turned into afternoon, Ben was beginning to wake up and level out. He had to pee, but could not. I guess it was something to do with his kidneys, but he tried and tried to use the hospital urine bottle but just could not. Ben ended up soiling himself and the bed from his straining. I looked at my son, lying in his own feces, coming off another overdose, and wondered what to do next. Because of his self-inflicted injuries, the doctors had no problems signing a 72-hour psychiatric hold to give me the time I needed to get things figured out.

Once Ben was stable, he was transported by ambulance back to Jackson and then literally placed in a padded cell. I hired yet another attorney to walk me through the process of having a person involuntarily committed to a drug rehabilitation facility. Ben would call us from the psych ward crying, begging us to get him out of there, and telling us about the poor souls who were confined in there with him. I told him I was sorry and that he could get out once we had a court order for a longer-term treatment facility. He cried even harder. "No, please, I don't need anything long term. I just messed up. Just send me back to Treatment Center #1 for a month." But we realized we might only have one more chance of helping him get well. Each episode with Ben continued to escalate, and we knew at some point he would not be able to survive another incident. Thus he needed to be at some treatment facility for longer than a month

We considered a couple of different options then ended up placing him at Treatment Center #2. This center is well known. It offers a 120-day dual diagnosis program, with the option of another 120 days of out patient therapy in a sober living facility they suggest. This was not a $5,000 28-day quick fix facility. This was the real deal, and the real deal cost $32,000 for the first 120 days, then about $10,000 for the next 120 days when he was ready to move to sober living.

Treatment Center #2 had four phases.

Phase I was basically a short acclimation phase. Depending on what drugs the person was detoxing from, this phase was generally just one or two weeks. Phase II was the balance of the first 90 days where the clients did group therapy several times a day, met with a counselor, and attended a few AA meetings as a group. They even did Equine Therapy a couple of times. One of the exercises they did involved having each client lead the horse through an obstacle course. The counselor would observe the technique each client used to accomplish the task. Ben later told us that if a client was rough with his horse--manhandled or maybe even slapped him to make him move--it might indicate that as a child the client was treated likewise. But Ben was very careful with his horse, patting it gently, encouraging it, saying, "Come on little buddy, you can do it little buddy." As you might guess, even horse therapy made me think we coddled Ben growing up and this whole mess was my fault. Joni even joked, "$32,000 in treatment, and even the horse blamed us."

I think I even once saw a Pepsi commercial that had me convinced I was the reason Ben struggled with drugs.

Phase III was where the client could come and go during the day. This allowed them to start working again, but every night they would have to return to Treatment Center #2 to get drug tested and sleep. Phase IV was outpatient therapy three times a week in the evening, and then clients could live on their own in a sober living facility.

Near the end of Phase II, Treatment Center #2 would offer Family Week.

Family Week was Monday-Friday, 8:00 a.m.-5:00 p.m. During this week 3-5 clients and their families would meet together and go through a series of exercises. One of the first exercises was for each client to make a list, year by year, that described their drug use that year, specifically what drugs they had used and how they got the money to support that use.

The first client out of the gate was Matthew, a 26-year-old architect from Virginia. Through our phone conversations and visits we learned Ben was closer to Matthew than anyone else at the facility. Ben and Matthew spent a great deal of time talking, and they had started studying the Bible together some. I really don't know how to describe Matthew's demeanor and countenance that could effectively picture what this guy looked like. He was defeated. There was no smile. There was no joy. There was nothing. Matthew was a good-looking guy, but he was one big blank stare. He did not laugh at jokes, he did not cry at pain, he was just the most defeated looking person I had ever seen in my life. He pulled out his multi-page list, faced his parents, and started reading and reading and reading. He went year by year through over a decade of hard-core drug use that culminated in needles upon needles full of heroin. It took him an hour to work through his list, all while facing his parents. His parents had a similar look of defeat. They were a very humble couple. They had worked hard to build a small nest egg, and they both looked very tired.

I recall at Treatment Center #1 thinking, *Well, at least we caught this early. Ben is not like these other guys who had to repeat rehab.* Now that we were repeating rehab, I recall thinking, *Well, at least Ben has never used a needle.* Hearing stories worse than Ben's somehow gave me a little hope that at least we had not gotten to that level.

The other three clients in the room with their families were all older than Ben, and all had worse stories to tell. Sam was from Dallas. His dad was a world-renowned scientist. His dad had done many of the same things I had done, and then some, to protect his son. The dad had even paid off drug dealers. That sounds insane, doesn't it? But I knew exactly why he did it. Like me, he hoped if he could get Sam over that one hump, just pour out his love on Sam one more time, hoping Sam would see how much he was loved and he would stop the insanity. So one of the most respected scientists in the world drove his son to the bowels of Dallas, gave his son $3,000, watched Sam walk away, and then waited patiently for him to return.

Sam did return, but he had been beaten to a pulp as a reminder of what happened when someone was late in paying their debt to a drug dealer. When the dad was driving Sam to Treatment Center #2 soon afterwards, they stopped at a hotel to spend the night. I don't recall if Sam had drugs with him or if he went out and found them. Regardless, Sam overdosed in the bathroom of the hotel room. His face was a bluish purple when his dad found him lying on the bathroom floor with a needle dangling from his arm. One of the world's most respected scientists found himself performing CPR on his own son in a hotel bathroom while stopped on their way, once again, to rehab.

Then there was Mr. New Jersey.

Large and in charge. Everyone just called him Jersey. His dad sat on one side of him and his pretty mom on the other. Money oozed from this family. Other clients, based on stories they had heard, concluded that the dad was some sort of mob boss in New Jersey. He owned millions in real estate and had beachfront vacation homes in their native country. Jersey was what some call a "high functioning" drug addict. He left New

Jersey to attend college at UCLA. He graduated and then opened his own restaurant. He had done great, but he had been high the whole time. And his habit had become expensive. Like any good businessman he kept records. Using an Excel spreadsheet he kept up with his drug use. In the twisted thinking of an addict, Jersey concluded that if he knew how much he was putting into his body, and how much money he was spending, and how to budget for future use, then he was in control of his addiction rather than it being in control of him. He drove a $70,000 Mercedes and was high from the time he woke up until the time he passed out every night.

He was not in control of anything.

In the room during Family Week sat four very different clients and four very different families. But the pain on each family was identical. We all listened to each client go through his using history. We all listened to each client describe how he funded his addiction, which, except for Mr. New Jersey, basically meant using his parents like an ATM. Afterward, the family members each gave feedback on how their son's comments made them feel, and whether we thought the client was being honest. We then listened to each client tell their family how they had been enabled in the past and then each client asked their family not to enable them in the future.

I thought this was such a crock!

The guys knew from their counseling sessions this was how they were supposed to feel, but it was a joke to think any of them actually felt that way. When Ben told the group how I got all of his charges either dropped or expunged, I replied, "Well, I can also make a call and have that undone. Want me to do that?" Of course, he did not. Sam told his parents if he relapsed he needed them to let him suffer the consequences. Everyone applauded him for his courage. When it was my turn to provide feedback, I told Sam that I did not believe a single lying word that came out of his mouth. I told him, "Sam, I don't believe a word of it. I think you just told your parents what you thought you were supposed to tell them in this session, but I don't for a second think that deep down you don't really hope that Daddy will come and rescue you again." Sam giggled, and said, "Yeah, well, I'm not sure."

Mr. New Jersey gave the same line to his parents, but he did not care. In my opinion he was just there to stay in the good graces so he could remain a part of the family fortune. I did not believe anything he said either.

Matthew, though, was different.

If Matthew had told me the sky was pink, I think I might have believed him. Matthew was broken. His parents were broken. Matthew was broken seeing his parents broken. The other clients were simply inconvenienced by their parent's brokenness. But Matthew sold me. And Matthew got honest. He did not want to be rescued any longer. If he relapsed, I could see in his eyes he wanted to die. I remember thinking to myself that he wanted to get well or get dead. He was tired of lying, he was tired of hurting, he was tired of hurting others, and he was just plain tired.

As a side note, Matthew was the only one of the four who did not relapse. He is doing great today, and I think there may be wedding bells in his not too distant future.

I think Family Week was where I first started to become jaded by the whole "rehab" thing.

I'm not saying rehab is wrong or does not work. But it is frustrating and even confusing that 100 different facilities have 100 different approaches and each is convinced their method is the best. But if this were true, they would have a success rate greater than 15 percent. The bottom line, above all else, is the addict has to want to get better. Nobody can make him or her better. Now I will say that once the addict wants to get better, if he has attended a quality treatment facility, he should have the tools to be able to get better.

In one session of Family Week, they talked about the pharmacology of addiction and tried to sell us on the disease concept. I bought into some of it, but still could not fully reconcile when choice became a disease. Nor could I understand how after being sober for an extended period of time, a disease could lead to another poor choice. You can cure a cancer patient even if they do not want to be cured, but you cannot cure an addict. I remember mentioning this to my pastor one day and he replied, "So where does Jesus fit into all of this?" Being a Christian, I wondered the same thing. Addiction was not a disease that forced itself upon you like cancer or diabetes. At some point everyone agrees it was a choice. So if your faith lies in the belief that Jesus can sustain you, that Jesus is stronger than any of your sick desires, that Jesus can fulfill the emptiness of your life, then where does He fit in? Ben believed in Jesus. So why did he not feel as if Jesus could meet all of his needs? Was it more of a spiritual issue for Ben rather than an addiction? Or did it start off as a spiritual issue and become an addiction? And once it becomes the disease of addiction, can spirituality cure it alone?

I had no answers.

I just felt like this whole rehab thing was a crock. But maybe that is too harsh a term. If so, at the very least, I felt traditional rehab was confusing. I did see benefit to rehab. I had heard testimonies of those who followed the treatment plan, followed the 12-steps of AA, gave themselves over to a higher power and stayed sober--but for some reason I still left Family Week feeling like I had been deceived through a $32,000 smoke and mirror charade. But on the flip side, it was worth every penny of the $32,000 to have Ben safe, fed, and in a program that at least made him evaluate his life.

I was truly torn and confused.

Chapter 16

He will turn the hearts of the fathers to their
children, and the hearts of the children to their
fathers, or else I will come and strike the land with
a curse. (MALACHI 4:6, NIV)

Near the end of Phase II, shortly after Family Week, Ben was allowed a
weekend off campus. We chose to spend the weekend at our deer camp. I
mentioned earlier that I joined the camp hoping I could spend countless
weekends with my boys there. I wanted to sit with them in the woods,
talk about everything and nothing, be quiet and listen, and enjoy God's
creation and beauty. Ben would always insist on bringing a friend when
he was younger. Being there with me did not really interest him. Michael
and I went often, but Ben did not--or when he did, he brought a friend.

But that weekend, for the first time I could actually remember, it was
just the three of us.

Just the way I had always pictured it. David and I not only share a
trailer at the deer camp, we also share places to hunt. Together we have
six food plots to hunt over (we each are allowed three) and about six tree
stands in the woods. Two of David's stands are close together, maybe
300 yards apart, so we decided to hunt there and each boy would take a
stand. So Ben, Michael, and I went into the woods around 3:00 in the

afternoon. I showed the boys where the trees were marked for them to go deeper into the woods and find each of their stands. They had radios so they could talk to each other, and let each other know (for safety) when either of them was coming out of the woods. I went back to the trailer to start working on our steak dinners.

I started out by marinating the steaks. I made my own marinade using olive oil, balsamic vinegar, soy sauce, lemon juice, garlic powder, onion powder, black pepper, and a large quantity of Montreal Steak Seasoning. While the steaks were sitting, I decided to make our three beds. I brought fresh linens from home since we had not slept there in quite awhile. I made my bed first, followed by Michael's top bunk, then I started making Ben's bottom bunk.

I have heard stories about something odd triggering an emotional response in a person. Maybe it is a smell that brings back a painful childhood memory. At times it is an article of clothing that brings back a painful memory of the loss of a loved one. For some reason, the act of making Ben's bed at deer camp, a place I longed for the three of us to spend time together, brought all of the emotions I had experienced over the last few years flooding into my mind and body.

As I knelt on my knees so I could reach across the lower bunk and spread the sheets smooth where Ben would soon sleep, I began to cry. I had not cried much at all over the last couple of years. I could not. I did not have time. Decisions always had to be made in the blink of an eye. Money was evaporating from my bank account, so I had to work harder to stop the bleeding. But I did not have time to work harder because of all of the meetings and counseling sessions we had to attend. Joni is a strong woman, but she would be the first to tell you she needs me. She does not want to face battles on her own; she wants me to be with her for strength and support. I try to budget time to let her know everything will be OK as well. I was staying up late working, working on weekends--since all of this started I think I just never found time to cry.

But there at Ben's bunk I began to cry.

I actually began to wail. I was crying and thanking and praising God for keeping Ben alive and bringing him to our deer camp that weekend. For over 20 minutes I was loudly and audibly wailing with thankfulness and gratitude, just wailing and praising and wailing and thanking and wailing and praising. Several years of pain, emotion, hurt, and even glimpses of joy came pouring out all at once, just because I was making Ben's bed.

In the Bible there is a story you may have heard.

It has been called The Prodigal Son or The Lost Son. The account is found in Luke 15:11-32. This short story is called a parable and is actually the third one in Chapter 15. To truly understand the context of the Parable of the Lost Son you must look at the first two verses of that chapter. "Now the tax collectors and 'sinners' were all gathering around to hear him. But the Pharisees and the teachers of the law muttered, 'This man welcomes sinners and eats with them'" (Luke 15:1-2, NIV). Jesus told the three parables because he was being criticized for associating with the tax collectors and sinners. Those who criticized him were Jewish religious leaders, who considered themselves righteous (in right standing with God) because they diligently and carefully worked to follow the laws of Moses. They couldn't understand how any respectable religious teacher would have anything to do with undesirable people like tax collectors and sinners.

The people Jesus most wanted to connect with--the lost and troubled of the world--frequently gathered to hear him and be with him. This is exactly what Jesus wanted to happen.

So Jesus took this opportunity to teach the people (especially the Pharisees), by telling three short stories that we call The Parable of the Lost Sheep, The Parable of the Lost Coin, and The Parable of the Lost Son.

In The Parable of the Lost Sheep Jesus described a shepherd who had 100 sheep, but lost one. The shepherd left the 99 sheep that were safe and went looking for the one that was lost. The shepherd rejoiced and celebrated finding the one lost sheep. Jesus then noted, "there will be more rejoicing in heaven over one sinner who repents than over ninety-nine righteous persons who do not need to repent" (Luke 15:7, NIV).

The Parable of the Lost Coin is very similar. A woman had ten silver coins, lost one, and thoroughly searched her whole house until she found the coin. She then invited the neighbors over for a party. Jesus again told the people who had gathered, "In the same way, I tell you, there is rejoicing in the presence of the angels of God over one sinner who repents" (Luke 15:10, NIV).

Then Jesus upped the ante.

He had already likened the joy of finding a sheep or finding a coin to the rejoicing in heaven over a lost sinner being found. Next he made it even more personal as he described a lost son returning to his father. The short version is a father had two sons. The younger son asked for and received his share of the inheritance and traveled to a distant land where he squandered his wealth in wild living. When he hit rock bottom, finally came to his senses and went back home, he was prepared to face the music and even become a servant in his father's house. But that didn't happen. The Bible says, "…while he was still a long way off, his father saw him and was filled with compassion for him; he ran to his son, threw his arms around him and kissed him" (Luke 15:20, NIV).

It was dark outside our trailer at deer camp and I heard Ben and Michael ride up on their ATVs. I walked out onto the porch and Ben saw I was crying, just like I cried again as I wrote this. Ben asked what was wrong, and I told him I had always dreamed of having my boys here at camp with me. I added that I had never been as happy in my life as I was at that moment. I hugged him and cried more, and more, and more. He could feel the pain being released from my body; he could feel the emotional torment I had endured escaping through my tears. He simply said, "I know. I'm sorry. I am here now."

There is more to the story of the lost son, however. Luke 15:23 tells what the father commanded after getting his son home: "Bring the fattened calf and kill it. Let's have a feast and celebrate."

That's what the father in the story did. And that's what we did as well. Ben, Michael and I had a feast, in the form of three-one pound Porterhouse steaks from Kroger. And I celebrated. But as I thought about the Parable of the Lost Son that night at deer camp, I also thought about the rest of the story. The other brother, who had stayed with the father, who had always done what the father asked, who had never disobeyed his father's orders, wondered why his brother received the choice gifts of time, attention, and possessions. I am sure Michael felt this way also. Michael was about to finish high school, but he would not be getting as nice of a truck as Ben got for his graduation. I could no longer afford it. If anyone ever deserved an overpriced extravagant high school graduation gift, it was Michael. But at this point, if you added up all of the costs for rehabs, emergency room visits, counselors, lost tuition, lost living expenses while attending school and failing, money Ben had stolen from us, and items stolen from our house by Ben's friends, it was in excess of $125,000. Michael, however, never got in trouble, never drank, and never did drugs. Still, he was going to have to pay for some of the cost by not getting as nice of a truck for graduation simply because we weren't able to do so.

Soon after our deer camp weekend, Ben entered Phase III of treatment, where he worked part time at an upscale commercial insurance firm. A very big-hearted member of our church created a part-time position for Ben, just so he would have a place to go, people to report to, responsibilities to fulfill, all while maintaining a flexible work schedule so he could attend the meetings and counseling sessions he needed to attend. He still reported back to Treatment Center #2 every afternoon, was drug tested, and slept there at night.

At the end of Phase III they counseled parents on good sober living housing options. It just so happened that the only one they suggest was an apartment complex owned by one of the owners of Treatment Center #2.

So Ben had reached Phase IV and moved into a sober living facility. Over the summer he took on more of a fulltime position at the insurance firm. He also went to three outpatient meetings a week in Phase IV. One day he came to me and wanted to talk about unfinished business: football. His eligibility was running out, and he was worried that the strain of having to get some classes under his belt just to become eligible for one year might not be worth it. But he wanted to prove to himself that he could continue to play football. He said, "Dad, remember that little Division III school that recruited me hard in high school, and the coach kept calling me and came to our house? I would give anything to even be asked to play for that school again."

So Daddy got on it.

Norman Joseph was the coach at the little Division III School called Mississippi College, located in Clinton, another suburb of Jackson. MC is a Christian school. So I called Norman, who also happened to be a friend of mine. I laid out Ben's whole story--the good, the bad, and the ugly. Norman asked how many semesters Ben actually finished versus how many he dropped out before completing. He got a little excited and said he needed to make a call and would call me back. Fifteen minutes later he called back and explained the eligibility clock in Division III is quite different than Division I. He said Ben had seven semesters of eligibility left at the Division III level, thus could play four entire football seasons.

So Daddy got into Daddy mode again.

Ben was doing great. He recommitted his life to Christ. He accompanied Joni, Michael, and me on a one-week mission trip to Haiti. He raised his hands to the Lord when he sang worship songs. The church asked him on Easter to take part in a musical presentation where he walked across the stage holding a sign giving God the glory for being 174 days clean and sober. He asked to be re-baptized on Mother's Day, and asked me to baptize him. He went to every meeting he was supposed to go to, he passed every random drug test he was given, and he was ready to start putting some of the pieces of his broken past back together.

I asked Ben one day, "Ben, tell me one thing I need to look for, one clue, one red flag that will alert me you are sliding in the wrong direction." Ben said, "That's easy. If I don't hit my knees first thing in the morning and stay close to God, then nothing else is going to fall into place."

Have you ever owned a fish tank?

If so, you know the water gets dirty every few weeks, and you have to do something about it for the fish to survive. If you take some of the dirty water out, but do not replace it with fresh water, things actually get worse. You still have dirty water, and algae starts growing on the side of the tank in the empty space where the water used to be. But if you take some of the dirty water out and fill the empty space with fresh water, your tank continues to thrive, your fish thrive, and algae does not grow on the sides.

Ben had worked really hard to get the dirty water out of him, and was filling the empty space with fresh water. He had fought hard to rid his mind of all of the bad things and was working hard to replace the bad things with the good things. He was spending time reading his Bible every day, he was praying, he was involved in our church and in our Life Group activities, and he was inviting others to be involved as well.

Consider this passage from Matthew 12:43-45 (NLT): When an evil spirit leaves a person, it goes into the desert, seeking rest, but finding none. Then it says, "I will return to the person I came from." So it returns and finds its former home empty, swept, and in order. Then the spirit finds seven other spirits more evil than itself, and they enter the person and live there. And so that person is worse off than before. That will be the experience of this evil generation.

Here is how I would translate this passage based on what we had been through for several years:

When an addict gets sober and rids himself of the daily evil usage of drugs and alcohol, it is like taking the dirty water out of the fish tank. If the addict does not replace that empty space, things will actually get worse. If a person does not fill the empty space with the things of God, the evil spirit, or in this case the addiction, will return seven times worse than before. Ben was right, if he ever quit hitting his knees, not only would the addiction return, but it would surely return at a level far worse than before.

But at that point Ben was doing great.

And what did Daddy always do when Ben was doing great? Daddy buys him a new truck, of course! I actually bought both Ben and Michael new trucks, which I could barely afford. But I was not about to let Ben get a nice new present without Michael getting something as nice or nicer. With Ben six months sober, I had not been wasting any money on ER visits or tuition, and I was able to honor both of my boys finally. And not only did Daddy buy Ben a truck, he helped him get admitted into school and bought his books.

Ben moved into the football dorm along with a good friend from church who was also transferring to MC to play football. But once again, the spiral began. First, Ben was not excited to be an MC Choctaw. Having been on the roster of two nationally known Division I programs, he just could not get excited about chanting, "One, two, three, Go Choctaws" at the end of a practice. Second, he could not remember the plays. His brain was still not clicking on all cylinders because of the extensive drug use over the previous few years. Third, he could not concentrate in class for the same reasons. Fourth, the peer pressure of being back in the college environment was greater than he anticipated.

As a result Ben quit football before the first game. He began missing class and eventually withdrew from school. He started using drugs again, and was living in his old bedroom in our house once again. He was beaten and defeated. It all happened so fast. But this time my compassion turned to anger.

Chapter 17

Pride  Aside

But if serving the Lord seems undesirable to you, then
choose for yourselves this day whom you will serve,
whether the gods your forefathers served beyond the
River, or the gods of the Amorites, in whose land you
are living. But as for me and my household, we will
serve the Lord. (Joshua 24:15, NIV)

So what should we do? Kick him out? Offer treatment again? For the first time since this started Joni and I were not on the same page. I just wanted him out, but Joni wanted to offer treatment. She said she could not live with herself if he died unless she felt like we had exhausted every avenue for saving him. But I just wanted him gone. Go live with Jeremy for all I care, which is where he had been staying and getting high for the previous week.

Remember Jeremy?

He was the high school friend with whom Ben had first started experimenting with cold medicine pills. He was now a full-blown addict. I even got a call from Jeremy's dad suggesting that he conduct "rehab" for Jeremy and Ben at their house. The dad tried to convince me Ben was not an addict; he just needed some guidance. The dad slurred through his oration, probably because he himself had been taking painkillers for years. He told me they were necessary to treat his aching back, which I am sure was a contributing factor. All I could think of was, *Seriously? Are you kidding me? Participate in a modified rehab at your house?* I politely declined his offer.

Reckoning day came once again.

We sat Ben down and told him he needed to go upstairs and pack his bags. He was leaving our house for good, never to return. I told him I personally just wanted him gone. "Go and figure it out on your own. Or go live with Jeremy and die high for all I care. Or join the military, except they probably do not want you either at this point. Or go to Colorado like the tens of thousands of other idiot addicts who think they want to live there since marijuana is now legal. I simply don't care, just pack your stuff and go."

I then told him Joni had begged me to offer treatment as an alternative. So although I did not want to spend another dime on him, except maybe to clean the carpet in his bedroom after he moved out so we could turn it into another nice guest room, I would be willing to buy him a one-way plane ticket to a facility in the Rocky Mountains several states away. Bottom line though, he was leaving right then, one way or another. He was either going to start walking down the street pulling a suitcase, or was going to take a one-way flight to treatment which would at least give him four months to eat and sleep and figure out what he was going to do after that.

Regardless, he was not coming back to our house.

By the way, this treatment center, a very beautiful one located in the majestic Rocky Mountains, cost $45,000. A friend helped us get a discount, and I sold Ben's pretty new truck to pay for some of it; even so, that was far more money than I had. But everyone said it was a great program that incorporated a wilderness aspect. There was hiking, riding mountain bikes, snow skiing, snowboarding, camping in the wilderness, all designed to help patients learn to have fun sober.

AARRRGHHH!!!

Life is not about having childish fun! Life is about moving past childish fun, and experiencing adult fun. Adult fun is finding God's purpose for your life, getting married, having a family, bearing children, buying a house, worshipping a living Savior, and finding contentment in all of the above. Adult fun involves strategy and work. If you work hard and live responsibly, then of course it is wonderful to be able to snowboard and hike. You have to find God's purpose for your life first and foremost in order to find happiness, not simply snowboard and hike to delay moving forward with the purpose for which God placed you on Earth.

I was angry. I was mad. I was fuming.

I wanted to physically hit him, but I knew I would end up getting the bad end of that deal. He detoxed in Jackson for three days before leaving for Treatment Center #3. I sat with him at the hospital in detox and did not sleep for two straight nights. He was begging every nurse that walked in to increase his meds and give him more dope. He begged every doctor to please increase his meds, that he needed more than they were giving him. Every 10 minutes he asked me when his next dose of medicine would be there. I went to get some food in the cafeteria and came back and saw him walking toward the front door of the hospital still hooked up to an IV. He had called his drug dealer, Big Hoss, and was meeting him at the front of the hospital to get some Xanax. I was able to talk him into going back to his room and he napped after that, but Big Hoss kept calling his cell phone. I finally answered, but Ben heard me giving Big Hoss a piece of my mind. Ben came out of the bed and attacked me slamming me up against a wall in his room. He grabbed an open Coke can and threw it at me, spraying Coke all over the room and me. I shouted down the hallway for the nurses to call security. Once everything had gotten calmed down and under control, I reached into my pocket and checked to see how much money I had on me, which totaled about $600 in cash. I calculated that we had about 20 more hours to spend in the hospital and gave the head of security $600 and asked him if he could post a guard with me in the room for $30 an hour. I was scared to be alone with Ben. I was scared of his rage. I was scared of my rage. And I was scared one of us would hurt the other before Ben boarded an airplane 20 hours later.

Why am I even trying to help him any longer? If he does not want to be sober, then why in the world am I killing myself trying to help him? Part of me thought I should just let him go. Everyone kept telling me, "He has not hit bottom yet; he has not hit bottom yet." All of the treatment centers talked about how addicts often want to get better after they have hit bottom. Everyone was telling me to let him go, to let him hit bottom, and then he would get well on his own once he hit bottom. In my opinion, this was also a crock. Ladies and gentleman, "bottom" is *dead*. That's what bottom is. So while part of me wanted to let him go so he could hit bottom, the other part of me knew without a doubt that bottom, at least for Ben, was death.

Eventually Ben got on the plane and was gone.

The doc gave him two doses of his detox meds to last him through the flight. I gave him about $20 cash to be able to eat during his layover.

What we did not know was that he had "cheeked" some of his meds at the hospital. In other words, he pretended to take his medicine by hiding it in his cheek, and then saved it so on the trip he could get good and high. Which he did. He not only took both doses they gave him for his trip, he also took all of the doses he had saved up. Oh, and at the DFW airport during his layover, he announced to everyone at the bar that he was on his way to rehab, and needed some folks to buy his final drinks before getting sober. Not only did several friendly fellow travelers buy him a few rounds of drinks, one particularly friendly business traveler shared some of his cocaine in the DFW bathroom. When he arrived at Treatment Center #3 Ben was completed loaded and the staff suggested he go through another medical detox so he would not be so uncomfortable. I suggested they shove him in a closet and let him sweat for a couple of days so he could learn what uncomfortable really felt like.

After a couple of days, Joni and I had a conference call with Kathy, his counselor at Treatment Center #3. Kathy was encouraging both of us to participate in weekly counseling calls and then come to Treatment Center #3 in a couple of months for Family Week. I explained to Kathy that I was done with all of this, and was not going to participate in anything. When we went through Family Week at Treatment Center #1 and #2, we were supposed to tell the boys that we were done, remember that? If they relapsed, we were supposed to be firm, hold our ground, let them go, and tell them we were done. We were supposed to tell them to go figure it out on their own. So I did not even want to send him to Treatment Center #3 in the first place. I did it for Joni.

I asked Kathy, "So tell me this, at your facility, during your version of Family Week, do you want the parents to communicate to the clients that they are done? If the client relapses, do not count on the parents any longer, right? Well if that is really true, and you teach that there, then you should fully expect me to be done right now, because I communicated that to him at the last rehab, and the one before that. I told him at the last one I was done, so how on earth could you ask me to participate if I am supposed to already be done?"

She got it; I was done.

She and Joni scheduled a time for the two of them to speak weekly.

I was done because I had to be right then to survive. I had just taken on a new project which would pay off some of the debt we were continuing to rack up, but I had to work long hours for 80 straight days with no days off. I not only wanted to be done, I needed to be done so I could focus on getting my life back in order, getting our finances back in order, and moving on.

After a week or so I started seeing calls on my caller ID from Treatment Center #3. I figured it was Ben, and I sent them all to voicemail. He would call Joni and talk to her, and always commented that he tried to call me and got voicemail. After 20 or so attempts, I guess he finally got the message that I had no desire to talk to him and no intention of taking his calls. Kathy sent me an email and said that Ben was hurt and confused as to why I would not talk to him, and maybe I should write him a letter to explain why I would not take his calls. I was happy to do so. Here is the letter I wrote Ben, verbatim, in its entirety:

Ben,

Here is the deal…

The main reason I don't want to talk right now is because I don't have time to talk right now. When you got on the plane, I have not had a day off since. I have worked 36 straight days and typically work from 6:00am to midnight every day, and sleep less than six hours a night. I am not going to let your crap affect this job. This is the most important project I have ever worked on in my life, and I am not going to let your decisions affect my work any longer. I spent the last four years working two hours a day and dealing with your crap the other 10 hours a day. I would work in the mornings until you decided to get out of bed and call me with whatever you needed that day…enroll in school, drop out of school, flunk a test, call a professor and ask forgiveness, bring you stuff you needed, etc. I spent more hours allowing you to manipulate me than I spent working, and that will never happen again.

Your drama is no longer going to affect me. I have been to family week or weekend twice already, and I am done with that. Me sitting in a chair and saying "your drug use has affected me negatively in the following ways…" is useless at this point. You know what you have done to us, and I am sick of talking about it. I don't wake up any longer and think about your drama. I now wake up and work my butt off trying to pay for your drama so I can hopefully replace Mom's 12-year-old car, and get her new countertops for the kitchen…that is now what is important to me.

I don't want to hear about how things are different this time. Just stay out there and do it. And when you finish there, go somewhere else and just do it again. If you want to get a degree, go find a college, meet with the financial aid people, and figure it out. If you want to get an apartment, go find a job, and figure out how to order electricity and water. If you can't figure it out, go join the Army and they will figure it out for you.

You told Mom that I "like" you when you do things my way and I don't like you when you don't do things my way. Well, you are full of crap. Quit acting like you are the victim. You caused all of this, not me. It's time you actually hurt and felt bad for real, instead of just going through the motions hoping Daddy will get you a truck and a job.

So what do you want from me? You want me to answer the phone and listen about your hiking adventure while I am in the middle of a 16-hour *workday? Are you freaking kidding me? Call me when you are in the middle of a 16-hour workday because you are trying to earn enough money to pay your cell phone bill. That's a conversation I might actually like to be a part of.*

A part of me dies every time I have to waste another hour of my life dealing with your crap. A part of me dies every time your mom doesn't want to face another day because of this crap and now ends up in the hospital because of it. A part of me dies when your mom cries because there are no presents for you under the Christmas tree again this year because you are in rehab. You want to call and chat about mountain biking? You want to call and chat about how you want to go spend more of my money because you think Pasadena would be a cool place to go? I don't want to hear it. Call me when you have a plan on how you are going to pay for your aftercare. Call me when you have a plan on how you are going to pay your Mississippi College loan. What step is it in AA when you make amends? Call me when you are serious about making amends to your mother and brother and all of the others who had to listen to your foul, vulgar mouth.

I love you more than my own life. I said many times I would die for you. Well, I have died for you. My soul and my spirit feel dead. I have died inside so many times inside I can't die any longer. If it weren't for my faith in Christ I wouldn't know how to live. If it weren't for my quiet time in the Bible daily, I wouldn't be able to face the day. I am so thankful I have that truth in my life so I can face the lies the world has to offer.

If you truly have something to say, I would answer the phone in a heartbeat. If you want to tell me about mountain biking and hiking, I couldn't care less.

So if I see a call from there, I will do everything I can to answer it from now on, because I will assume you have something to say. Otherwise, no need for you to call me. Dad.

He never called…I guess he had nothing to say.

Then Christmas rolled around. This was his second Christmas in rehab. Last Christmas, when Ben was at Treatment Center #2, Joni and I joked about what our Christmas card would look like.

I love doing Christmas cards every year.

I keep a list on my computer and update it every year. My parents were good about doing Christmas cards, but my grandparents were even better. When I was little we would go to my grandparent's farm in the Ozarks and they would have hundreds of Christmas cards on display from people they knew from all over the country. I loved that. And I still love sending Christmas cards to this day. So every year we would plan our family photo. One year it was in front of our Christmas decorations in our front yard. One year it was in a golf cart when I was working at the PGA TOUR event. One year it was at a beautiful setting off of the Natchez Trace, which runs from Nashville, Tennessee to Natchez, Mississippi.

But what would we do this year for our annual Christmas card picture? Would we all gather in front of the rehab sign for a photo? I sarcastically mentioned to Joni maybe we should take four individual pictures and put those on the card. I joked that it could be like the Brady Bunch, just little squares on a card like the Brady Bunch Tic Tac Toe graphic at the opening of the show where everybody looks left, right, up and down at each other. Joni and I continued to joke about how perfect that would be since we were *such* a Brady Bunch family. Joni and I kept joking and talking about it though, and came up with an idea. If you counted our dogs, cats, guinea pigs, and fish, we had enough Huttons to fill up the Brady Bunch Tic Tac Toe board. Our caption could even make light of the fact that we were not the perfect family, but had chosen to put *Pride Aside*, and move forward anyway. So we did. Some of us looked up and some of us looked down like Jan and Marsha. Some of us looked left and some of us looked right like Peter and Bobby. We even posed the animals to look left, right, up, or down, and we created our Hutton Bunch Christmas card, with the following caption and Scripture.

No longer trying to be America's perfect family!
"Faith is being sure of what we hope for and certain of what
we do not see" Hebrews 11:1
Merry Christmas from our Beautiful Mess to Yours

But that was last Christmas.

Now we were spending another Christmas with Ben off in rehab, and I was mad. I was just mad, pretty much at everyone. We sent Ben a Christmas gift. He asked for a digital camera so he could take pictures of the beautiful Rocky Mountain scenery at Treatment Center #3 while he hiked and mountain biked and learned that being sober could be fun! Ben's girlfriend (who we absolutely adored) wanted to take several pictures so when he turned the camera on there would already be some great pictures from home on the disk. The camera could also record video like most digital cameras can nowadays. I decided to film a short video, a little song parody I performed for him, partially out of humor, and partially out of anger. So I strummed my guitar, and sang him a sarcastically re-written parody to *Christmas in Dixie*.

Christmas in rehab
Two years in a row
First Mississippi
Now New Mexico

Merry Christmas in rehab
Enjoy your short stay
Mom misses you dearly
And Michael says "hey"

But did I really feel this way?

Or was I just putting on an act because I was supposed to feel like I should let him go? I still do not know the answer to that. I know I really did have those feelings of anger on the surface. But deep down, I wanted my boy back. I wanted the Ben back that I had taken a mission trip with in Haiti. I wanted the Ben that I was with at deer camp. I wanted the Ben back that followed me with a toy lawnmower. Deep down I wanted Ben back, but in order to survive personally, I needed to take a strong posture of no longer caring.

So, how was Joni during this time?

Not good. In my letter to Ben I mentioned Joni was struggling and ended up in the hospital. That was true. The mind is a powerful tool. It can pull you out of horrible situations, or it can shut your body down in stressful situations. Joni was admitted to the hospital with severe medical symptoms. Her head felt like it was about to explode. She had tingling in her face and extremities. Was it a tumor? Was it a stroke? Was it stress? She was not doing well. I had spent two nights with no sleep during Ben's detox, and then weeks of endless work to pay the bills, and now Joni's body was shutting down from stress and she needed her husband.

And who was checking on Michael during this time?

Was he OK? How was he coping? Did he need both of us? He had just entered Basic Training in the United States Air Force. He was hospitalized on his first day at Basic. He was experiencing stress related medical symptoms and was in a hospital in San Antonio, Texas. Our whole family was imploding. Our whole family was dying. I wanted to cut our losses and let Ben go, but I also wanted my son back.

I remember searching the Scriptures looking for some sort of peace, some sort of hope in what seemed like a hopeless point in my life. I grabbed my Bible and read from the book of Job and was comforted when Job lost his family and all of his possessions and yet he still cried out and said, "Naked I came from my mother's womb, and naked I will depart. The Lord gave and Lord has taken away; may the name of the Lord be praised" (Job 1:21, NIV). I was comforted when I read, "However, if you suffer as a Christian, do not be ashamed, but praise God that you bear that name" (1Peter 4:16, NIV).

But how could I comfort Joni?

How could I comfort Michael?

Could we all heal and move on if Ben would just go ahead and die? Or if Ben did die, would Joni die with him? Would Michael die with him? What was I supposed to be doing? Was I supposed to be fighting for Ben? Or was I supposed to be fighting for Joni and Michael? How could I possibly fight for all of them? And how could I hold Joni's life together and Michael's life together when my life was spiraling out of control just as fast as their lives were?

Chapter 18

Pride  Aside

Is anyone crying for help? God is listening, ready to
rescue you. If your heart is broken, you'll find God
right there; if you're kicked in the gut, he'll help
you catch your breath. Disciples so often get into
trouble; still, God is there every time.
(Psalm 34:17-19, MSG)

My phone rang. You guessed it. It was 2:00 a.m. This time it was Ben
calling.

Ben had completed treatment at Treatment Center #3 in January of
2013. He moved from the Rocky Mountains to the Smoky Mountains
into a recommended sober living facility I will just call Sober Living.
Sober Living was recommended by Treatment Center #3, and Sober
Living also operated from the premise that all you had to do was show
guys they could have fun being sober, and life would work out. Sober
Living charged $8,000 for the first month, and then $3,000 per month
thereafter. Oh, but they got to go snowboarding all of the time, and had
family meals together, and went to concerts so all of the clients could
learn how to have fun sober. Anyway, after Ben had been at Sober Living
for a month or so I made a trip up there to see him. I bought him a bed,
since he was sleeping on an air mattress at the sober living facility. It

was really hard for him to find a job because he was at the mercy of the community van used at the sober living house to ferry clients to work and appointments. So I bought him another piece of junk car, a 10-year-old Ford Explorer with over 100,000 miles on it so he could apply for jobs.

He ended up working full time at a telemarketing call center. Can you imagine a worse job in the world than being a telemarketer? Taking a list of numbers and cold calling people and being hung up on or cussed out for eight hours a day?

However, Ben was actually good at it.

I guess one of the things he had picked up from me over the years was the gift of gab. He could sell ice to an Eskimo. He could sell hay to a farmer. He could sell plastic surgery to Joan Rivers. He could sell religion to the Pope. OK, I will stop, but he really was good at selling. The telemarketing company was selling tickets to a benefit concert for children burn victims. That right there is a much easier sell than a Ginsu knife, but still it was a little shady. The company gave Ben a script, which looked like an organizational chart. The top of the chart had his opening question, and depending on how the person on the other end of the call answered, would depend on whether Ben responded with the follow-up question on the left or the follow-up question on the right. Regardless of how the person answered, Ben had a script for what his next response should be. After awhile it became second nature to him. A sample call might sound something like this...

"Hey, this is Ben calling on behalf of the _____ Volunteer Fire Department. (Oh, and by the way, he was instructed to speak like a hick redneck to authenticate the part). How is your day going today? Ha Ha Ha, well that's great (regardless of how they responded), well the reason I am calling...."

You probably understand because you've received similar calls. Anyway, it was a job, and he was doing it well. He had a knack for keeping people on the phone longer than others, then selling them tickets to an upcoming concert benefitting burn victims. He was making a good hourly wage, was consistently getting bonuses for above average sales, and was even asked to consider a management position one day. It made him feel good about himself to know that he had a marketable trade: he could sell.

Meanwhile Michael, our youngest son, had received what is called an ELS discharge from the Air Force. The doctors determined he had documentable medical symptoms such as excruciating leg pain and partial paralysis. But while the pain and the paralysis were real, there was no medical reason they should be occurring. The doctors likened it to West Nile, but he tested negative for West Nile. Whether it was mind or body we will never know, but the bottom line was, the pain and paralysis were real and he could not train. An ELS discharge is an Entry Level Separation. It simply means the Air Force turns back the hands of time and pretends like he never enlisted. This is a good thing as far as discharges go. A Medical Discharge often prevents an enlistee from returning to the military, but with an ELS discharge, he could one day return to the military if he desired. Michael had enlisted to become a MP, or Military Policeman (the Air Force calls it Security Forces or SF). After time as an SF, he wanted to become a civilian policeman, and continue as an SF in the National Guard. And while a SF career was no longer on the table, he still wanted to pursue a law enforcement career, so my contacts with local law enforcement would help him pursue his dream.

Michael applied for dispatcher positions with Ridgeland PD and Madison PD, and a Detention Officer position with the Madison County Sheriff's Office. I lined up meetings with friends in each agency. Michael met with the Ridgeland Police Chief, the Madison Assistant Police Chief, and the Sheriff of Madison County. While he waited for an opening to occur in one of the three agencies, I worked out an arrangement for him to start performing "ride alongs" with the Madison PD. On March 15, Michael put on some black BDUs, a black turtleneck, a black police duty belt with handcuffs and handcuff case, a vinyl glove pouch, and a flashlight and went riding with one of the shift sergeants. You could not slap the grin off that boy's face.

But like I said, my phone rang at 2:00 a.m., and it was Ben.

"Jeremy is dead, he killed himself."

"He was at his house and went out by the pool and shot himself in the head." Jeremy's dad had died just a few months before. Jeremy had spiraled downward ever since his father's death. Jeremy had actually been with his father on a tropical island off the coast of South America. Jeremy's father had always had a dream of retiring in such a place, and Jeremy and his dad were on the island doing work to the future retirement home when the dad passed away. Jeremy took their boat to the mainland to seek assistance, but the officials said there was nothing they could do since the island was not in their jurisdiction. They said Jeremy needed to go back to the island and retrieve his father's body by himself. Jeremy returned to the island, loaded his father's body onto a boat, and took him to the mainland. But after returning to the United States, Jeremy spiraled out of control. Ben and Jeremy had often talked in the past about how both of them needed to get sober and quit all of their mess. Jeremy tried once or twice, but never tried very hard. Ben loved Jeremy, and just prior to Jeremy's death had even talked to him at length about trying to get sober and seeking treatment. Ben was devastated at the news. He sounded broken over the phone.

Once again, death had reared its ugly head in close proximity to our oldest son.

What never occurred to us was that the first call Michael would ever go on while riding with Madison PD was to a call of "shots fired" at an eloquent residence in a gated subdivision on the west side of town. After realizing that the shot fired was of a self-inflicted gunshot and there was no immediate danger, none of the responding officers were on high alert. They were there just to document the scene. Michael never let on that the place was familiar to him as he walked through the house, onto the back porch, and out to the pool area where Jeremy was dead with a bullet wound to the left side of his head. That was Michael's first introduction to what a lifetime of law enforcement might look like, lying there in the form of Ben's best friend, Ben's first using buddy, the kid who spent the night with us dozens of times, the kid who visited church with us often in middle school, the kid who Ben took his first ski trip with, the friend Ben had just recently begged to get sober. There was Jeremy, a victim of drugs and depression. There was no note. Jeremy was high and in a fit of rage, and simply walked outside of his house and declared his disease cured as he pulled the trigger.

About 100 days later, Brad Taggart, the 12-year-old baseball teammate of Ben's and son to Andy Taggart, the former Chief of Staff for Governor Kirk Fordice, also placed a handgun to his head. Brad however did leave a note to his precious family. The note was an oxymoron. Webster's defines an oxymoron as "a combination of words that have opposite or very different meanings." Brad described his feelings in one way, but the beauty of his prose had an opposite or different meaning. He said he had lost his mind due to drugs--drugs had robbed him of his memory and the knowledge he had gained, he had zero reading comprehension skills and an attention span of about 10 seconds, and he had no emotion. He added that he spent the majority of the day staring off into space, and felt like he had fallen into a psychosis. He said he could not control the voices in his head and that he slept all day, not because he was tired, but because he hated being in reality. He said he wished he could disappear unnoticed, that he had no hope. But yet it was obvious that none of what he wrote was true. His letter was elegant, it flowed well, and had perfect grammar and punctuation. It looked like it was written by a Rhodes Scholar with great forethought, insight, and emotion.

But Satan had convinced Brad otherwise.

The enemy had stolen Brad's hope, and convinced him that his progression from marijuana to cocaine, to ecstasy, to mushrooms, and to LSD had ruined his life forever. Brad did not pull the trigger on the handgun in the Taggart's front yard that July morning, but Satan himself murdered Brad. It was premeditated over months of spiraling drug use. How ironic it was when Brad's toxicology report later came back clean, further proving that this brave young man was trying to fight the battle of addiction on his own, hoping to free himself from drug use and Satan's grip.

This next part is difficult for me to describe.

I just do not know if I can craft the words effectively to paint a picture of what I witnessed in person. I earlier described Andy's wife, Brad's mom, as an eloquently beautiful woman. She is far beyond that. Her physical beauty is obvious. She is tall and carries herself gracefully. Her eyes are deep and her smile is perfect. In the South we say when a guy like Andy marries a woman like her that he "out punted his coverage." Her outer beauty is unmatched, however, to her inner beauty. Karen is such a godly woman, sweet in spirit, and deep in wisdom. She serves as a perfect helpmate to Andy, and as a perfect "boy-mom"--allowing fish guts in the sink and smelly clothes in the hamper.

But at visitation on the day before Brad's funeral, there was only one way I could possibly describe Karen. She looked like she, too, had suffered death, but yet was still breathing. There were thousands who had gathered at our church that evening to pay their respects to the Taggart family. The line was so long that after three hours the decision was made for the family to walk down the receiving line and thank the remaining visitors for coming. The family needed to put an end to a grueling day. Andy and the boys assisted Karen down the line, as she was unable to stand without collapsing. Her face was unrecognizable, being filled with grief, pain, torment, and tears. But it was more than that, and this is what is hard for me to describe. There was a look of confusion, honest and utter confusion. Her face screamed, "Why am I here? Why are all of you here standing in line? Has anyone seen Brad? I am sure he is around here somewhere. I think the boys are planning a duck hunting trip this fall." The look of pain and confusion on Karen's face was one I had never seen before, but would see once again in the near future, and that would be on Ben's face.

I will tell you about that shortly.

Chapter 19

Pride  Aside

Whoever loves money never has money enough;
whoever loves the wealth is never satisfied with his
income. This too is meaningless.
(ECCLESIASTES 5:10, NIV)

By this time I had read a dozen or so books trying to learn more about Ben's disease, or his choices, depending on which camp you prefer. I continued to feel like it was primarily a disease when he was in active relapse and use. I also continued to feel like it was primarily a choice when he had a significant amount of sober time under his belt. So like a left-leaning conservative or a right-leaning liberal, I sat squarely in between the two aisles and would lean left or right depending on what was going on that day.

I first read the Alcoholics Anonymous book, or the AA book, or the Big Book as they sometimes call it. It was written in 1939 by Bill Wilson, whom most refer to as Bill W, and Dr. Bob Smith, known simply as Dr. Bob. I studied the "12 Steps" and was fascinated by the first three:

1. We admitted we were powerless over <u>alcohol</u> (I substituted <u>drugs</u> in Ben's case) and that our lives had become unmanageable.

2. Came to believe that a Power greater than ourselves could restore us to sanity.

3. Made a decision to turn our will and our lives over to the care of God as we understood Him.

The next nine steps are really just action steps after you have come to terms with the first three. The next nine action steps include things like taking personal inventories of your actions, making amends to those you harmed, and helping other alcoholics/addicts do the same. I read the whole book, cover to cover, but kept coming back to the first three steps, which, if you truly think about it, are simply steps to analyze your spiritual condition.

My biggest surprise in reading the Big Book was in learning that the entire program is really a spiritual program. I felt Ben had a good grasp of step #1. He readily admitted that when he was using, his life was completely unmanageable. There was no argument; he had come to that conclusion several times, which for you or me would probably be enough to keep us from ever wanting to use again. So this first step would cause me to lean back to the disease theory side. Why else would someone continually relapse? If they knew the result would once again be an unmanageable life, it would be literally insane for them to relapse.

Ah, insane. Which leads to step #2.

How does a person not feel insane any longer? Step #2 says to believe in a Power greater than yourself, which in our house and in our family meant giving your heart and your life to Jesus Christ. Ben had done that as a child, and just to remove any doubt in his mind, he had done it again a little over a year earlier as he recommitted his life to Christ and was baptized again on Mother's Day. Step #3. *Made a decision to turn our will and our lives over to the care of God as we understood him.* Houston, we have a problem! How can you possibly move on to steps 4-12 if you cannot get past step #3? Ben knew his life was unmanageable. Ben believed in a Holy Father who sent a loving Savior. But not for a second had he given his life over to anyone.

Next I searched for books written by fathers who had an addict child. *Beautiful Boy* and *Clean* were both written by David Sheff. As I read *Beautiful Boy*, about David's son Nic, I knew what was going to happen in the next chapter before even reading it. There were so many similarities between Nic's story and Ben's story. Nic eventually wrote a book himself called *Tweak*, and I read it hoping to get a glimpse of addiction from Ben's perspective. The biggest difference between my and Ben's story and David's and Nic's story seemed to be that both David and Nic were atheist (as near as I could tell) or agnostic at best. Nic once said, and I paraphrase, that finally at the urging of his sponsor he prayed to a Heavenly Father he did not believe in. He even started off his prayer by saying even though he did not believe in him (God), he had a list of things he needed some help with. I guess that would be like going up to a man on the street and saying, "I know for certain you are not my real father, but here is a list of needs I really need you to meet for me," and then be shocked when it does not happen.

I also read a book called *Broken* by William "Cope" Moyers, the son of the famous Bill Moyers who was press secretary to President Lyndon Baines Johnson, a network news commentator for a decade, and had spent the balance of his life in public broadcasting. Cope talked a great deal about living in his father's shadow--never feeling like he could be as good or possibly one day even outshine his father. I am no celebrity, and in my opinion my life does not cast a very deep shadow, but it made me wonder if I had ever made Ben feel inadequate. Cope finally stayed sober, after coming to grips with step #3. He finally sought long-term treatment, and stopped believing he could stay sober on his own. We had always tried to get Ben to accept long-term treatment, but he always wanted to get out as fast as he could because, like most 22-year-olds, he felt he could do it on his own.

Ben came home from Sober Living to attend Jeremy's funeral.

His world once again had been rocked by the death of a close friend, this time a lifelong friend and fellow user. At the funeral, half the mourners were stoned, which disgusted Ben. You would assume that something as sobering as Jeremy's death would make an addict stop using forever, never thinking about allowing any poison to adulterate his mind or body ever again. And for most people that would be true. For Ben, he thought at that moment it would be true for him as well. He had often struggled in his own mind whether he wanted to "be the good guy or bad guy." He once told me that early in high school he recalled having a conversation with himself. He literally thought it through. *Do I want to be one of the good kids, go to church, be kind to others, study hard, make good grades, and please my parents? Or do I want to be one of the bad kids, push the envelope, experiment with sex and drugs and alcohol and see what level of fun that might bring, and be tough and mean-spirited at times to prove that I'm bad?* He actually recalls the day he thought about which road he would take, when he said to himself, "Forget it, I'm going to have fun."

But after all of his experimentations, his football and school failures at Southern Miss, Ole Miss, Mississippi State, and Mississippi College, his time spent in emergency rooms, treatment facilities, and psych wards, it came down to the moment of attending Jeremy's funeral. Ben once again confirmed to himself that enough is enough. He had been sober this time about four months, and asked us if we would support him moving home and getting a job. He wanted to stay with us for a few weeks until he started getting a good paycheck and found a place to live. We agreed. We came up with a list of the same old guidelines and rules from before. You have to be in AA and go to meetings. You have to meet and check in with your sponsor. You have to be home at normal times so we do not sit up and worry. You have to take drug tests. You have to go to counseling.

So he packed up his piece-of-junk Ford Explorer with all of his worldly possessions, and he came back home.

Not only had our Life Group at church rallied around us, so had others who had heard our story. They often told us how we had inspired them just by being open and honest about what was going on. This was a difficult balance to strike. Regardless of Ben's decisions and setbacks, I did not, repeat, did NOT want to shame him through the things we did or said about his situation. We struck a very delicate balance of dealing with our own feelings and emotions as we were truthful and honest about the struggle we were facing, but at the same time we were very careful not to harm Ben's feelings or dishonor him in any way. Whenever Joni and I would speak to a class about what was going on or have dinner with a family who was worried about their child, we would tell Ben about it, and often get his permission before speaking publicly. Even this book was not published until Ben had a chance to read it from cover to cover and make sure he agreed with all of the facts presented.

Greg is a member in our church. We know Greg and he knows us, but just well enough to recognize each other in the grocery store. Greg is the general manager of the big Ford dealership in town. He was willing to give Ben an opportunity to work selling cars. The car business attracts a variety of applicants. Although there are some talented people in it, let's be honest, its reputation unfortunately is that of a place people go when they cannot do much else. Maybe they had a good job and lost it, so they decided to sell cars. It is a shame this reputation is still so prevalent, but it exists. Greg despises this reputation, and for good reason. Nowadays, especially at most large dealerships, there is a quality staff so this reputation is not true. In fact, Greg always seeks sharp, go-getter young men and women who want to build a successful career. He even works with a local university to create a flow of strong, business minded students who would like to use the car business as the starting point for their career rather than just a fallback.

So Greg gave Ben a job.

Did I mention Ben could sell ice to an Eskimo? Well, since the Ford F-150 is the best selling truck in America, this job came pretty easy to him. Ben did well. He trained for a month or two to learn the products and the procedures. Then he sold nine cars his first full month flying solo. Then he sold nine more the next month. He loved it. He stayed late on the days he should come home early. He went in on his one weekday off to meet a client almost every week if necessary. He dropped by on a couple of Sundays when the dealership was closed just to give his card to a few would-be shoppers who were milling around. Every time we went out to eat, he struck up a car conversation with the waiter or waitress and gave them his card. He was eating and breathing his new career. It's like he was addicted to it.

Wait--like he was addicted to it?

Yes, it really was like that. It was like he had traded one addiction for another. I had to think about that some. Maybe, if you have an addictive personality, you just get addicted to things. Anything is a possibility. Back in my PGA TOUR days, we had John Daly playing at our event every year. John has had his fair share of substance abuse issues. One year we got him a house at the Country Club to stay in since the homeowners were out of town. I went into the house after the event to make sure he had not wrecked the place. I found 13 empty boxes of Lucky Charms! Everyone on TOUR said he was always addicted to something, and I guess that week it was Lucky Charms. Maybe someone can get so addicted to a good thing that it actually can be harmful. Work can be a good thing, but too much can be harmful. But let's look a little deeper.

In drug use, you are not addicted to the swallowing of the pill. You are not addicted to the actual sticking a needle in your arm. You are addicted to the effect it gives you. You are addicted to the high it provides after you've put the pill in your mouth or squeezed the liquid from a syringe into your vein. Maybe Ben was not addicted to the work itself, but from the effect it gave him. The effect of being a good car salesman is having a wad of money in your wallet. That was new to Ben, and he seemed to be hooked on it.

He seemed to be so hooked on it that he wanted more and more and more. All of the guys at the car dealership passed the time on rainy days, or on sunny days when they just did not feel like going out and working the lot, by gambling online. Aren't smart phones wonderful? You can sit at your desk, give an online company your credit card number, and gamble all day. Now gambling is stupid enough in and of itself. But at least if you are actually sitting at a blackjack table in a smoky casino you can see the cards get shuffled. Or if you are throwing dice at least you actually get to see the dice tumble down the table and come up snake eyes. But who on earth would gamble on their phone and wonder why they did not win? Have you ever heard of a big winner on their iPhone app?

So that was how the sales guys passed their time. Once the gambling bug had bitten Ben firmly, he wanted to hit a casino. It amazes me how easy it is to type out the steps to another relapse and see where they are heading. Why on earth is it so hard for an addict to see the progression as it is occurring in real time?

Here is how it goes:

1. Trade your drug of choice for a new drug of choice, in this case, money.

2. Instead of being productive in your idle time by following up on old leads, or creating new leads, you sit around the dealership and play blackjack on your iPhone.

3. Justify that you can go to a casino as long as you go with friends who hold you accountable so that you do not consume the free alcohol.

4. Win a few times, and lose a few times. But only remember and focus on the times you won and block out the times you lost. Win, $2,000. Come home with $0. When asked how you did, tell everyone about the $2,000 jackpot and leave out the part about you leaving with $0. Also leave out the part about the additional $500 in ATM withdrawals.

5. Sneak back over to the casino by yourself to try and make some of the money back that you lost. Lose even more. Lose about $4,000, the total amount you had saved up since starting back to work.

6. Now, feeling like a complete and total failure and idiot, drink some of the free alcohol.

7. Go back to work and feel like the biggest loser who ever had graced the car lot. Borrow a couple of Xanax from the guy who takes them regularly, but still functions, at least for a while on the job.

8. Get paid, and instead of paying your rent or buying your groceries, dial up your old drug dealer who you have not spoken to since your dad answered the phone in the hospital, and score some more Xanax.

9. Call in sick a few times because you stayed up all night getting high, because the more Xanax you took, the more you felt like a failure, thus requiring even more Xanax.

10. Have your dad try to find you when he realizes you are missing work, and he finally finds you stoned, sitting in the corner of Henry's trashed out apartment, another one of your old using buddies, as you sit there and contemplate how you have blown it all again.

You see, when an addict relapses, he usually does not start out at Henry's trashed out apartment getting high. He does not even start out by calling his former drug dealer. He usually starts out by doing something very casual, almost innocent. This is why for many addicts, going to AA meetings every day for accountability, talking with their AA sponsor, and spending their idle time with others in recovery is so critical. But you must be willing to submit yourself to that level of accountability. You have to want to stop, period. This means you have to put some barriers in place and respect those barriers. But Ben was not willing to do those things. This is all purely my opinion, and not what Ben said, but I do not think at that point in time he truly wanted to stop. He just wanted to find a level where he could use and not spiral completely out of control--which is insane considering his history.

I took him to a hotel that night.

Ben and I were in a unique new stage of our relationship. He no longer was afraid for me to see him high. He hated it. He would constantly say he did not want me to see him like that and ask why I kept trying to help him, but he no longer hid the fact that he was in turmoil. So why did I keep helping him? I had come to a conclusion that death was bottom, and that Ben was going to reach bottom either on that relapse, or maybe the next, or possibly the next, but soon he would die reaching his bottom. I had decided during that relapse that I was going to continue to walk this journey with him, as long as I was physically and mentally able, and as long as Joni and Michael were physically and mentally able.

Ben went back to work, started going to a few meetings, and tried to stay sober on his own. Ben had gambled away any possibility of finding a roommate and finding a house or an apartment to rent, so this put us once again in a difficult situation. We would not tolerate Ben being high in our house, so he needed to go. But at the same time, he had nowhere to go. His boss at work was very sympathetic to his struggle, but in order to protect the work environment he placed Ben on leave and told him his job would still be waiting for him when he was well. After a day or two of struggling with what he should do next and struggling to stay sober, Ben came out to my office.

That was the only other time I have seen a face in pain and turmoil and confusion like I saw in the face of Karen Taggart at Brad's visitation. Ben was crying and wailing and hurting in a way I had never witnessed before. He told me how he felt his mind was going insane. He shared obsessive thoughts that would flood his mind that he could not shake loose. He tried to explain more, but with every sentence he spoke, the look of confusion increased in his face, the look of despair and hopelessness became deeper and darker. He said, "I don't want to do this stuff any more, but I can't get these thoughts out of my head. I can't concentrate at work. I will have a simple form to fill out and it will take two hours because all of these horrible images and thoughts are just flooding my head. I can't work. I can't sleep. I feel like I have two options, put a gun to my head or get high. Help me get these thoughts out of my head and I won't want to get high."

I wonder if that was what Brad was feeling as he penned his suicide note. I wonder if that was what Jeremy was feeling as he walked out of his house and out to the pool with a gun in his hand. I wonder if that is what all addicts feel, seeing as how Step #2 specifically talks about restoring their sanity. I asked Ben which came first, the thoughts or the drug use. Had he suffered these thoughts and they were what led to drug use, or had the drug use caused the feelings of insanity? Even though he felt like these thoughts went back to high school, they were obviously not as intense back then, and never caused the pain and hurt I witnessed on his face that day in my office.

I had an entirely new appreciation (or perhaps understanding might be a better word) for what Ben was going through after that morning. I felt his pain like I had never felt it before, because I saw it in his face like I had never seen it before. I came to several conclusions that day, which complicated things even more for me.

- Nobody wanted this to stop more than Ben did. He was tired, worn out, and sick of living the way he was living.
- Nobody else saw his face and felt his pain the way I did that day. All of the advice from treatment centers, counselors, and other addicts about what to do would still be considered, but ultimately he trusted me at that point. Thus I needed to put careful thought and prayer into every future plan.
- I needed to acknowledge the counselor's observation that he and I had a co-dependent relationship, and try to help my son live while at the same time placing boundaries to protect me and give him the space to get well on his own.
- He was sick. On that day and at that time it was a disease. I needed to remember that fact and base my actions and suggestions on the fact that it was a disease, just like cancer.

- He needed to consider medical and psychiatric assistance in addition to traditional addiction solutions.

- We needed to guide him toward a deeper connection to God, so he could once again feel hope, and we needed to pray that hope would lead him to a point of wanting to continue to fight. We knew ultimately we could not force him to connect with God; we could only pray for him and offer guidance during teachable moments.

It was around Labor Day.

I found a highly recommended psychiatrist in town who Ben felt comfortable meeting with. The psychiatrist also was on the fence about which came first, the chicken or the egg: Did the OCD, manic-depressive, bi-polar type thoughts and symptoms cause Ben to abuse Xanax and other drugs, or did the abuse bring on the symptoms? A couple of the treatment centers Ben had attended were considered to be dual-diagnosis centers, which means they also try to determine if there is a chemical imbalance or mental illness that might be a contributing factor. The difficult part of discovering this is that the person has to be sober for quite some time to be able to separate and analyze what is drug related and what is underlying. Ben had been sober four months one time, eight months one time, and four months the last time. But he had never gotten a year or two under his belt to be able to determine a good baseline diagnosis. The psychiatrist wanted to put Ben on some medications to help even out his highs and lows. We also set him up with a Christian counselor so he could begin a dialog about how he was feeling.

My big work project was cranking back into high gear. This gave Ben an opportunity to work for me doing mundane manual labor to keep him busy and provide a few dollars to put gas in his car. The project, which was in its second year, was to build an outdoor ice rink in Madison for the community to enjoy during the Christmas season. It was a huge success the first year drawing 105,000 visitors from all over Mississippi and beyond. We spent $200,000 in lights and trees and decorations. Every night we had concerts featuring church choirs and school choirs singing Christmas music. There was a party pavilion where we hosted 375 children's birthday parties. There were live television and radio remotes and broadcasts. Building the event took a couple of months, and Ben was able to help with that. He constructed and painted thousands of linear feet of picket fencing and helped put trees and decorations in place. It kept him busy, but he was not feeling any better.

He was secretly sneaking Adderall and Vyvanse in addition to the medicines the psychiatrist had prescribed him, which basically nullified any chance of allowing the proper medicines to work. His highs and lows continued, and his anger and rage began to return. He wanted to run. Addicts always want to run. Part of them feels like all they need to snap out of it is a new start, or new scenery, or new friends. I think deep down they want to run because they know every move they make is being watched closely, every word they speak is being critiqued, and if they can get away from that, they can go a few weeks or months fooling a new set of friends.

Ben made a call and got his old job back in the Smoky Mountains. He convinced himself that he could go there, get back into Sober Living, and be fine. Before he left, Ben and I went and got him a new iPhone with a new number, trying to put a barrier between him and his problems in Mississippi. I told him I would keep his old phone to use as a spare in case Joni, Michael, or I got a cracked screen and needed a replacement. He told a mixture of truth and lies to his former roommate at Sober Living who was over a year sober and still had Ben's old room empty. The truth he told, at least what Ben truly believed was the truth at the time, was that he needed to be back there and get back in a routine of daily devotions, meetings, and accountability. The lie he told was that he was sober and had been sober, but still felt like he needed to get some things back on track.

Ben did great for about a week.

But misery loves company I guess. After Jeremy's death, Ben's new using buddy was Henry, the same Henry whose trashed out apartment I had found Ben cowering in a few weeks earlier. As you may recall, Ben had tried to convince Jeremy to seek treatment just before his death. Because that didn't happen, Ben felt like he fell short. Now Henry was not doing well. Ben did not want to lose another friend, so he talked to Henry about joining him in the Smokies so they could get sober together. Henry loaded up his vehicle the following week and drove from Mississippi to be with Ben. Henry took his clothes, his fishing gear (since Ben told him about the great fly fishing opportunities there), and his toiletries. Oh, and he also took all the dope he could get his hands on to make the transition to sobriety smoother. When Henry arrived, the days and weeks that followed would take Ben to his lowest of lows to that point. Within eight weeks Ben would twice knock on the door of the ultimate bottom and look at death face to face once again.

Chapter 20

Pride  Aside

Everyone who practices sin also practices
lawlessness: and sin is lawlessness.
(1 John 3:4, NASB)

Ben's old phone sat on my desk. I had never deactivated it from our account, and I watched as text messages still came through to his old phone. Some were messages that people were sending to his old number, not realizing he had a new phone number. One was his dealer, Big Hoss, who I mentioned earlier. I do have one little confession to make right here. Since Big Hoss did not know Ben had a new phone, and since I thought Ben was safe from retribution in the Smokies, I decided to have a little fun with this thug. I texted him from Ben's phone and said, "Hey, this is Ben's dad, I see you have been texting. I guess you did not hear that Ben died of an overdose recently. We just got Ben's phone back from the coroner, and just wanted to let all of his friends know that didn't know." Big Hoss immediately called Ben's number, and cried out, "Is this Ben's dad? Oh, tell me it ain't true, man. Put Ben on the phone man, just put Ben on the phone. I told him don't be messin' with that stuff no more. Who gave him that stuff, man? Don't be messin' with me, man, just put Ben on the phone man, just put Ben on the phone." I told him how nice it was for him to call, and it sounded like he was a true friend to Ben, and

I hated to have to break the news to him. So I had a little fun with Big Hoss.

I have since heard he is in jail.

Some of the messages on the old phone were iMessages, however, and I could also see the response Ben was sending from his new phone. Here is a short technology lesson. When you own Apple products, like an iPhone, iPad, or iMac computer, you can enable a feature called iMessage. This is an Apple enabled text messaging system that can be linked to all of your Apple devices by signing in with your Apple ID. So if you get a new iPhone, iPad, or iMac, and sign in with your old Apple ID, any device that is still logged in under that same Apple ID will continue to receive iMessages from other Apple users.

I knew this full well when I bought Ben his new phone. I assumed he thought if the phone was in my name, I could still access things, so I even set the phone up in his name alone, and told him it was time for him to have his own account so I could not meddle in his affairs. But I made sure he logged into his new phone using his old Apple ID, so he could retrieve his contacts, photos, and apps. What he thought was a gracious gift was actually a ploy to monitor as many messages and emails as I could. Using his old phone I was able to see every conversation he had with anyone else who used iMessage--which was most of his friends. I could also see every email he sent or received. All of his old apps were still enabled like Facebook and a couple of secret chat apps, so I could see Facebook messages and more. Ben is a very smart guy. He always knew that I monitored things as best I could. Thus he always was cautious in what he communicated to others and occasionally found alternate means of communication. Not for a second did I think I was completely fooling him; he was way too smart for that. But if I did not let on to everything

I was seeing, I hoped I could get a few bits of information on what and how he was doing.

Had I achieved the ultimate level of co-dependence?

Of course I had. I was just as sick as he was, but in a different way. Was I aware of that? Did I know that? Did I even have a couple of people point that out to me? Yes, Yes, and Yes. Did I have any intention of stopping? No. Monitoring Ben was not hurting or enabling Ben, it was only hurting me. But I did not care because I thought it might somehow save him in the long run. I felt like this might be a secret weapon I could use to head off Ben's death, so I was going to use it.

In addition, I still had a couple of pieces of leverage.

His car was in my name. If I saw he was using, I could go get the car. I could inform his sober roommate who would have to take action to remove Ben from the house. I planned to use what leverage I had left to try to make him uncomfortable enough to possibly return to treatment before he hit bottom. But I still did not believe in sitting by and just waiting on him to hit bottom, because bottom was dead.

Within a matter of days, it was evident that Ben and Henry were on a binge. Ben was trying to make deals. He was texting dealers as well as guys he had met in recovery who were no longer in recovery. The end of his run was obviously near because of the urgency of his text messages. He probably was out of money and out of dope. It looked like he had bartered anything he had of value, like golf clubs and Dr. Dre's Beats headphones. So he was getting panicky. I did not want to tip my hand, but at the same time I wanted to talk to him to see if he might be ready to stop. I called him and asked him where he was. He lied, so I just said, "Ben, look, you are trying to meet a dealer. Hey man, it's all gone down hill for you real fast. Why don't you just stop? Go home, stop, and let's see about getting you some help." He said OK, he would go home, but then he immediately started texting the dealer again. It was late and I was exhausted just watching the exchange, so I went to sleep.

The next morning I called one of Ben's friends to see if he could give me an update about what was going on. Ben had been arrested a few minutes after we spoke the night before on a felony cocaine charge and a misdemeanor marijuana charge. For those keeping score, this made his 5th arrest and his 9th and 10th charges. But this was his first felony, and a felony sticks around for life. There will always be a little box on the job application that will haunt him. He cannot carry a firearm, which means he can no longer go hunting. This was a life changing moment. Would it be the wake up call that made him want to stop?

And what about me?

What should I do now? Should I help him? I really did not think so at that point. I thought I should advise him on how to help himself. But as bad as I wanted to save him, I knew he had to want to save himself from himself. All of my efforts to help up to that point had been for two reasons--to keep him alive and to keep him from making a life-long mistake that might cause him to feel he had no more reason to live. I feared this might be the proverbial nail in his coffin, but I had to let him figure it out.

We spoke the next day, which was Sunday, and he was supposed to make an initial appearance in court Monday. Ben was coming off a pretty good binge, but he had no money. Henry was out of dope, and so Ben was freaking out. Ben had not been staying with his sober roommate, but instead had been crashing on another user's couch. His sober roommate told Ben he loved him, but he knew the drill--Ben could not live in his house for at least a month or two until he had some sober time. Ben's car had been impounded so he had no way to get to court, but the sober roommate was nice enough to drop him off. Ben was so anxious he was actually scared to go into the courthouse. He was texting me sporadically, and we spoke for a few minutes. But he was either high again (somehow) or he was just freaking out so badly he did not make sense. He texted me several times once in the courtroom saying he had to get out of there. He could not handle it and he just had to get out of there. I kept telling him he had to hang in there, make his appearance, plead not guilty, and ask for a public defender if he ever wanted any relief from this felony charge. It was his first charge of any kind in North Carolina. Courts do not want to give jail time for first time offenders with a small amount of cocaine; they just want them to get some help. I kept telling him simply to make his appearance, get a public defender, find out what was required to reduce the charge, go to treatment or whatever they told him to do, get rid of the felony, and then, move on. But he was freaking out. He said he threw up in the courtroom and left. He simply texted and said, "I can't handle this," and left the courtroom.

While all of this was going on I called a crisis hotline I found in North Carolina on the Internet. The nice lady told me there were hospitals he could go to in the area that would accept him. She gave me the name of one of the hospitals. I sent a text to Ben with the hotline number and the name of the hospital. I told him he might want to consider calling the number or going to the hospital since he had no money, no car, and no place to go. He never responded. I called him. It went straight to voicemail. I had no idea if he had seen my messages before his phone went dead.

I really felt like I had spoken to him for the last time.

Joni and I both sensed that was it. We sent an email to a few friends saying we had lost contact with Ben and asking them to pray. I got a message from his sober ex-roommate saying he heard some guys had given him a ride to the hospital, so I guessed he got my last text. They also said he left the hospital and walked away. That was all we knew.

About 20 hours went by and he finally called, just to say he was alive and would call again later. He had walked about eight miles back to the guy's house where he had been staying. His sober roommate went to talk to Ben and laid out his options. Since Ben missed court, he needed to go back as soon as possible, explain he threw up and freaked out, and see if he could set another appearance. Ben did so and was assigned a public defender. But then he had to find a way to live for about three weeks until he went to his final court date. I sent the sober roommate money, and he provided Ben food but not much else. Ben tried to stay sober for three weeks, went to meetings, and just sat on the couch all day since his car was still in the impound lot.

By this time there was a new person he started texting, a girl who lived in Madison. She also had a few issues, but nothing like Ben's. Ben told her about getting in trouble and said he was ready to get away. Again, the addict was ready to run. He still had no idea I could see his correspondence, or at least he did not realize I could see both sides of the conversation. He always knew I could see some things; he was not clueless by any means. So whenever I would text him or talk to him, I would just encourage him to stay sober until court, meet with his public defender, do what the court suggested, and he could get the felony reduced. He did those things but continued to plan with this girl to move to Los Angeles. They traded emails about housing. She had lived there for a while and knew some people who could help Ben get a job selling cars. I did not let on that I knew; I just kept watching this ridiculous exchange as they planned their move to LA. I saw emails where Ben was telling potential employers what a great salesman he was, how he loved his current job (which was a lie since he did not have a current job) and how he was just looking for a change by moving out west.

His court date finally arrived.

He handled it all on his own. He met with his public defender and the court agreed to reduce the charge, but Ben had to agree to go to drug counseling and complete treatment within a year. If he met all of those conditions, the cocaine charge would be expunged.

But Ben was still ready to run.

He stayed with it long enough to get court behind him, but I suppose he was ready to go surf in the Pacific. I finally called him and showed some of my cards. I basically asked him, "So when you move to LA are you going to take my car, or are you going to be nice enough to drop it off in Mississippi along the way?" He did not ask how I knew and he did not argue. He just said, "I will drop it off for you if you want me to. I don't want to ask you for anything else." I already had sent his sober roommate money a couple of weeks before. The roommate had gotten the car out of the impound lot so it would not continue to rack up charges. I told him to give Ben the keys. I suggested to Ben that he stay in the town he was in, get a job, and get back into recovery. What I did not know was that Ben had scrounged up some drugs and sold them to make some money. Because he had some money, he was already using again and had decided to move up to heroin. He had avoided needles up to that point in his life, but he was planning to take that next step.

He kept scheming to move to LA. He told the girl that because he smoked some weed (he didn't tell her about the cocaine and heroin) that his roommate had kicked him out and his parents had cut him off. When she bad-talked Joni and me for cutting him off and told him what horrible parents we were for not giving our angel child a second chance for one little slip up, Ben defended us and said we were just trying to do the right thing. I was proud that he stood up for us. (I guess I was looking for things about Ben to be proud of.) She talked her parents into wiring Ben $400 so he could get back to Madison, where her parents said he could move in with them temporarily. I did not let on that I knew he was coming back. I did remind him that if he ever wanted treatment we would pay for it, otherwise we would not send him another dime.

He made it to Madison and moved in with the girl's family. The girl bragged to Ben how she and her mom manipulated the dad so that he didn't ask any difficult questions. I wanted so badly to warn the father before Ben moved into their upscale home. But I did not. The girl's dad knew who Ben was, and he could look me up in the phone book and verify Ben's story. But he never did. I decided not to intervene but just to let it play out. I already was doing more than I should have been doing by monitoring his communications. At least I was holding firm to offering treatment only and no other support. The girl's mom even got Ben a job at one of the retail locations of the company she worked for. On Ben's first day of work he reported in at 10:00 a.m. but quit before lunch by just walking out. His drugs were gone, he was sick, and he felt like he needed a fix. What he really needed, however, was treatment or whatever it would take for him to get long-term sober time.

Chapter 21

Pride  Aside

We know what real love is because Jesus gave up his
life for us. So we also ought to give up our lives for
our brothers and sisters. (1 JOHN 3:16, NLT)

My phone rang again, but guess what? It was NOT 2:00 a.m. It was a
Friday afternoon. And it was Ben. He simply asked, "Is it too late to ask
for help?" I replied, "Ben, I will always help you seek recovery." He did
not want to take any more of our money. He knew we had eclipsed the
$200,000 mark of spending on him from the costs of treatment and lost
money from schools and doctors. He knew the house we once had 60%
equity in currently had a $200,000 second mortgage. I told him I knew
about a treatment center not too far away that was very inexpensive and I
had the money to pay for it. I also said he did not need a treatment center
next to the ski slopes; he just needed to WANT to get sober.

I keep coming back to the disease versus choice debate.

I guess I did that because it is the biggest mystery of any addict's story.
By now, Ben wanted to be sober. So why was he constantly relapsing?
Nobody wanted this to be over more than Ben. So again, the constant
relapsing lent credibility to the disease theory. Something would cause
a trigger, something would make him anxious or scared or uneasy, and
the disease knew that the one thing that could make the feeling go away

was to use. It takes a great deal of sober time to be able to find coping mechanisms that help the addict get past those feelings without using. So in this sense, I should not have been so jaded about treatment centers. While none of them have the answer, and they all use different methods, the one common denominator is they are trying to help the addict cope so he or she can attain sober time. The more sober time the addict racks up, the easier it becomes to use coping mechanisms rather than using drugs or alcohol.

I reminded Ben that it seemed like he always was ready to get help late on a stinkin' Friday afternoon when there was nothing we could do until Monday!

Argh!

He could not go back to the girl's house because he was too embarrassed that he walked out of the job her mother had gotten for him. All of his clothes were at her house except for a few items he had in his car. So I got him a room for two nights at the hotel he always went to when he had no other place to stay. I gave him some $25 restaurant gift cards so he could eat. I told him if he drove himself to treatment on Monday that he could call me and I would come pay for it.

This was where I got really jaded about the whole "are you enabling" process. I was getting advice from every different direction: "Let him go." "It's up to him." "He needs to check himself into treatment on his own." OK, OK, I knew that; I really did. I fully understood if he did not want help, anything forced or coerced would have little effect. I understood it was up to him.

But I also understood I was the one he came to when he wanted help. By staying involved in the process and by keeping in touch with him, I was able to maintain a rapport with him so when he was ready for help, he just picked up the phone and called me. The balance I justified in my mind was to withhold any financial assistance unless it was related to recovery. But I would still meddle in his business as much as I could from a distance, seeking to know how I could guide him when he was open to guidance. Most "experts" say do not meddle--cut them loose and let them figure it out. I do not think, however, I prolonged his suffering and using by monitoring from a distance what he was doing. Had I been providing him a place to live, utilities, and gasoline while he was in active relapse, then I would have been prolonging his suffering and usage because that would enable him to be comfortable and use spare money for drugs. I felt like there had to be a balance. Was I making myself sicker by staying so emotionally connected to him? Absolutely. And if I could have taken his addiction and placed it in my body and healed him completely, I would have done so. If I could have removed every craving, every withdrawal symptom, and every compulsive thought that went through his mind and placed it on me, I would have done it.

That is what my Heavenly Father did for me.

Over 2,000 years ago, God looked down from Heaven and saw the sin of the world--the sin of all those who had ever lived as well as the sin that would be committed by all future generations--including you and me today. He took all the burden of sin from humanity and placed it on himself. God became man in the form of Jesus Christ. He came to Earth in a physical body and lived a sinless life, then died a horrible, sacrificial death on a cross so our sin could be removed and forgiven. By believing in Christ, and placing our trust and faith in Him, we can be assured that one day we will live in eternity in Heaven alongside Him. Although God provided this sacrifice--this avenue to eternal life--we still have to act. God will walk 99 steps toward us to try to draw us into a relationship with

Himself, but He does not come that 100th step. We have to act. We have to take one step toward Him in order to be saved from an eternal Hell.

I saw the pain in Ben's face.

I took 99 steps toward him by monitoring his actions, staying in touch, and offering treatment. I tried to show him the love of Jesus by forgiving him while guiding him. But I knew he needed to take the one step to free himself.

Monday morning came. Joni went to work and Ben dropped by the house on his way to check himself into treatment. He asked if I wanted to drive him there. On one shoulder I had this voice speaking to me saying, "Yes, drive him, he is willing to go, take him there." Then I had a bunch of voices on the other shoulder saying to me, "Let him go; it's up to him." I told him to go ahead and drive himself, and if he got checked in to give me a call and I would drive down and pay for it.

So off he drove, straight to his drug dealer.

He had somehow scraped up a few dollars from somewhere. If I had driven with him, I assume he would not have asked to stop at his dealer's house. But I did not, and he did. He bought 13 Xanax. He called me and texted me a couple of times trying to figure out directions to the rehab. He let me know he was there, so I finished up a few things at the house and started making the drive to Treatment Center #4 to pay for his entry.

When I arrived, Ben was sitting in the waiting room so high he could barely speak. The staff indicated that they would not accept him into treatment until he had been detoxed for two to three days. They also said that Ben had told them that he had taken six or seven Xanax, which for some people could be a lethal dose. The male nurse said, "Mr. Hutton, we think he needs to get to an emergency room." I replied, "I totally agree,

I hope he can figure out how to get there." I took the keys to Ben's car, looked Ben in his glazed, distant eyes, assuming he would not be able to comprehend or remember what I was about to say. I hoped that somehow he would. I said, "Ben, they said you can't come back until you are sober, so if you decide to come back, give me a call, and I will come pay for it."

I walked out the door.

The male nurse followed me into the parking lot and said, "Mr. Hutton, I know you are just trying to do the right thing by not enabling him, but considering the situation, we think it would be OK for you to take him to the emergency room." I thought this was funny. The "experts" at the treatment center, who usually are very matter of fact in their preaching against enabling and letting the addict suffer the consequences of their mistakes, suddenly went against their timeless advice simply because they did not want to have to deal with him or be responsible for him. So I walked back in, grabbed Ben, and put him in my car.

There was no reason to talk to him on the drive to the hospital. He was loaded, and this was not a teachable moment. He would not remember any of it anyway. We got to the hospital ER that was the same hospital he detoxed in prior to going to Treatment Center #3. While he nodded in and out, I pulled out a note pad and drew a map. I placed the ER in one corner of the map, and Treatment Center #4 in the other corner, and drew the main roads between the ER and Treatment Center #4 and also placed a few well-known landmarks along the way. I got him out of the Yukon, and took him to the back of the vehicle, and pulled out his rolling duffle bag. His whole world had basically been reduced to the contents of that rolling duffle bag. I had the car back, all of his clothing and possessions were at a girl's house, and all he had was in this bag. I took the map and showed it to him, "Ben. Ben. Look at this. This is a map to rehab. You are here at the hospital, and the rehab is here. If you get sober, you can walk from the hospital to the rehab and check yourself in. If you check yourself in, call me, and I will come pay for it. Do you hear me? Do you understand?" He nodded and gave me a big hug and said thank you. He then asked where he was supposed to go. I pointed to the door of the ER. "Ben, do you see that door with the big Red Cross over the door? Go in that door, and later if you check yourself into rehab, call me, and I will pay for it." It was 33 degrees outside and the light rain was turning into sleet. Ben hugged me again and walked toward the door of the ER. I drove off, and called Joni. She too felt like we had done all we could do at that point. She reassured me it was time to let him go. I broke into tears as I drove away.

I felt so helpless.

We had been through enough situations like this to know that more than likely another 2:00 a.m. call was going to come. So I slept in the guest room that night trying to protect Joni from hearing what drama might unfold. But it started sooner than I expected. Ben called around 10:00 p.m. and said the emergency room personnel had come to two conclusions. Even though six or seven Xanax would kill some people, he was in no danger of dying and did not need to be admitted. They further decided that, since he had not been using very much over the last week or so, he did not need to be detoxed. They asked him to leave the hospital. So the phone rang, it was Ben, "Hey, the hospital kicked me out, can you come get me?"

I cannot explain to you how much I wanted to go get my son.

The temperature was hovering around freezing, rain mixed with sleet was pelting down, and Ben had already walked from the ER to a gas station pulling his wheeled duffle bag to ask to use the phone. He was wet, freezing, and alone in the "hood." The hospital he walked away from was in the one of the worst areas of Jackson, filled with drug dealers and gang members. A stoned preppie boy from the suburbs pulling a wheeled duffle bag had to look like an easy target. We had left him alone in jail cells, we had withheld finances and left him alone in other cities and other states, but none of those experiences ever seemed to be the magic bullet to make him want to stop using.

"No, Ben, I can't come get you. Find a warm place to sleep. I am sorry, but no, I cannot come get you. Do you still have that map? If you can find your way back to rehab and check yourself in, give me a call, and I will come pay for it."

I tried to sleep.

I was able to doze off and on, but then he called me again. "Dad, hey, I am totally lost, I have no idea where I am, can you come find me?" I replied, "No, Ben, I can't come find you. Find a warm place to sleep. I am sorry, but no, I cannot come find you. Do you still have that map? If you can find your way back to rehab and check yourself in, give me a call, and I will come pay for it."

Next came the 2:00 a.m. phone call. It went like this:

Ben: Dad, don't freak out, OK? But I have been shot in the head.

Me: OK, Ben, well where are you now?

Ben: I am at the hospital.

Me: At the same hospital you were at before?

Ben: I don't think so; I think it is a different one.

Me: How did you get there?

Ben: An ambulance came and got me after I was shot.

Me: So there are doctors and nurses and everything all around you?

You are inside? Checked in? They are taking care of you? Or are you just outside the hospital?

Ben: I am inside, there are doctors here, they let me use the phone.

Me: Ok, so you are safe, and they are taking care of you?

Ben: Yeah, I got jumped and robbed, and they shot me in the head.

Me: OK, do you still have that map? If you can find your way back to rehab and check yourself in, give me a call, and I will come pay for it.

Then I hung up.

I know. I know. You are wondering about him being shot in the head, right? Well I was wondering also. But I figured if he was in the ER and was able to use the phone and to talk to me, then he was OK. If it was life threatening I assume someone else would have gotten on the phone and talked to me.

Next came a 3:00 a.m. phone call:

Ben: Dad, they don't know what the (Bad Word) they are doing here. They are not giving me the medicine I need. They gave me Tylenol. I am getting out of here. This is ridiculous.

Me: OK, do you still have that map? If you can find your way back to rehab and check yourself in, give me a call, and I will come pay for it.

That was the last call of the evening. I slept. Joni went to work the next morning. I hopped in the shower around 8:00 a.m. and just as I did, my phone rang. The caller ID said Madison Police Department. I hopped back out and answered the phone simply by saying, "Is my boy alive?" The officer said yes, but he had been found unconscious at a gas station near the interstate. I told the officer, "Man, I am glad he's alive, and I appreciate you calling, but do whatever you need to do; I don't want to come up there." The officer said, "Well he isn't in any trouble, he was just asleep at the gas station. The paramedics are here checking him out, but we really can't get much information out of him. Is there anything that you can share with the paramedics that might be helpful?" I told the officer I would be there in five minutes and tell the paramedics everything I was aware of if that would be helpful.

When I got there Ben was sitting up in a chair. He had no recollection of any of the events from the night before. So I told the paramedics the story as best I knew it. They deemed him fine. But now, once again, I was faced with the question of what to do with him? It was Tuesday morning. I knew from the past that after what he had just experienced, with so much Xanax still in his system, he would probably sleep for the next 24 hours straight. So I called the rehab, told them the sequence of events, and they agreed to let him check in Wednesday morning if we watched him for 24 hours and made sure he did not take anything else. I dumped him into the back of my Yukon, drove him home, then dumped him into the guest bedroom. His wheeled duffle bag had been stolen, so his total belongings consisted of the jeans he was wearing, the shirt on his back, and my borrowed tennis shoes on his feet.

He did sleep all day Tuesday and into the night. Joni went to bed in our bedroom and I slept in my chair in the living room so I could hear if Ben woke up and came out of the guest room. He did wake up around 3:00 a.m. and wandered into the kitchen. I also got up and went in there. Ben got something to drink out of the refrigerator then sat down at the kitchen bar.

This was the dialogue that followed:

Ben: Do you have the keys to my car? I want to go outside and get a smoke. You can come with me; I'm not going to do anything.

Me: Ben, your car is at the rehab place. We left it there when you went to the hospital.

Ben: Where is my duffle bag?

Me: Ben, remember, you said you were jumped and robbed last night, and that you were shot in the head.

Ben looked at me with a very confused look on his face. He thought for about 20-30 seconds as if he were replaying the entire night in his head. Then he slowly reached his hand up to the back of his head and felt the large knot and crusted dried blood stuck in his hair. He looked at me and asked, "That was real?"

As he thought more about it, bits and pieces began to come back to him, so he told me the story. After the second phone call to me when he was lost and calling from a gas station, he started walking in the freezing rain, pulling his wheeled duffle bag down the street. He came across a kid and asked where he could get some dope. The kid hung with him for a little while. Ben thought the kid made a call on his cell. In a few minutes, as the two of them approached an intersection, three guys got out of a vehicle and jumped Ben at gunpoint. They took his wallet, his duffle, and beat him in the process. As they finished, the guy with the gun drew it back and smashed it across the side of Ben's head, and the gun went off. Whether it was the slide of the gun or the bullet itself that put a crease down the side of Ben's skull, we will never know, and it does not matter. They left him there, and Ben ran to another gas station holding his bleeding head and told them he had been shot. Ben also realized the remaining Xanax he had were not still hidden under the sole of his borrowed tennis shoes.

So at some point during the night he had taken the balance of the pills, which means he had taken a total of 13 Xanax, normally a fatal dose for anybody.

We didn't talk much more; he was in deep thought trying to put the pieces together from the night before. I told him the rehab agreed to accept him in a few hours and suggested he get some more sleep.

This time I would drive him there.

When morning broke, I filled Joni in on what all had transpired while she slept. Then she was off to work. How she kept managing to get up and go to work I will never know, but I was proud of her strength and courage. She spent a lot of time reading her Bible to draw strength, a lot of time in prayer, and a lot of time with our Life Group friends for support. I was very proud of her then; and I still am today. She always was and still is the best boy-mom I have ever known, even with all of our struggles.

Ben's clothes were still at the girl's house in Madison. The family had not heard from Ben in several days, so the dad finally reached out and called me. I told him the whole story. I also told him I had considered reaching out first but it was their business, not mine. The dad said he knew something was not right, and had talked to his wife and daughter about calling me but they talked him out of it. Regardless, he was kind enough to bring all of Ben's clothes to our house while Ben was still asleep.

Ben finally got up that morning.

We found another piece of luggage and packed it with some of his old clothes from his bedroom. It was a quiet drive to the rehab. He apologized numerous times along the way. I told him I knew full well nobody wanted it to be over more than him. He had dodged a near overdose once again and had dodged a bullet, literally. I asked him if he remembered how he got from the hospital to Madison. He said he did remember, but he did not want to tell me. Since the statute of limitations for borrowing certain items without permission may last awhile, I will not say any more about how he got from Jackson to Madison. I will say, however, that I made sure that if there had been a certain borrowed item, that it was back in the right person's possession and undamaged.

On the drive we talked about all he had been through. We discussed how maybe God allowed him to go through all of this so he could help so many others down the road. I told him he had developed quite a testimony, but I thought he had enough of a testimony now so he did not need to add to it any longer.

At one point Ben said to me, "Pops, you should write a book. With everything we have been through you should have plenty of stuff to fill a book." To which I replied, "Ben, I tell you what. I will write that book, under one condition. It has to have a happy ending. I don't want to write the book unless it has a happy ending."

Chapter 22

Pride  Aside

*In all their distress he too was distressed, and the
angel of his presence saved them. In his love and
mercy he redeemed them; he lifted them up and
carried them all the days of old.*

(Isaiah 63:9, NIV)

So here we are, at the end of the book. Does it have a happy ending? Here
is what I have come to realize. Every night that my two boys, Ben and
Michael go to sleep still breathing, it is a happy ending to that day.

As I type this final chapter, I am sitting in my blue leather chair in
our den. It is Father's Day 2014. Joni is napping on the couch. Our
awkward 75-pound, 11-month-old adopted puppy Rebel (see, I have
nothing against the Ole Miss Rebels!) is gnawing on something; I think
it is the couch Joni is napping on. Michael is asleep upstairs because he
worked the midnight shift last night as a Booking/Detention Officer at
the Madison County Sheriff's Office. But Ben is not with us today. He is
with us, in the sense that he is still breathing, but he is not physically at
our house in Madison today.

What you have read are simply bumps in the road that have occurred
in our life. Every family has bumps in the road. Some are great, some
are good, and some are not so good. I will say this. I have typed
approximately 60,000 words so far as I have explained some of the not-

so-good moments in our lives. But if I started right now typing all of the wonderful events that have occurred in our lives, I would be at 6,000,000 words in the first chapter alone.

I am a blessed man--blessed beyond measure--and I do not deserve any of the blessings I have received. Joni is a wonderful woman, a wonderful wife, and a wonderful mom. She tolerates, no she embraces my entrepreneurial spirit and just rolls her eyes and smiles when I come home every few months or years with a new venture I am about to undertake. I mentioned a couple of times that she is the perfect boy-mom. She keeps our house very up to date, very pretty, and very clean. Yet she does not freak out when she discovers a rut in the yard from a truck that missed the driveway, or when she smells a five-pound catfish that has just been placed in the freezer on top of the ground round and ice cream containers, or when she sees the leg of what appears to be a large pre-historic bird in the floorboard of one her son's truck. I don't think we ever got the full scoop on that one.

I am SO proud of my son Michael.

Michael has endured a lot with our family; but through it all, he stayed true to who he is, Whose he is, and what he has always wanted to become. Michael has always had a passion for all things military and all things law enforcement. He excelled in high school ROTC and in the Civil Air Patrol. He worked his way through the ranks of both organizations and received numerous awards and honors along the way. He solo piloted an airplane at age 16. He finished high school early so he could enlist in the Air Force. Although he was unable to complete training and was discharged, he still is steadfastly pursuing a career in law enforcement, and loves his current position as Detention Officer with the Madison County Sheriff's Office. He is working hard and training and one day plans to be on the road as a policeman or a deputy sheriff. I am SO proud of him. By the way, he looks so stinking good in uniform. Everything he has witnessed over the last few years has not been in vain. He wants to use the fire that has been built up inside of him and hopefully work with a narcotics department one day.

As much as I am proud of Michael, I am equally as proud of Ben.

Can you possibly imagine how tired you would be if you had walked in Ben's shoes for the last five years? Yet he continues to fight. Who could do that? Who could wake up after multiple setbacks and multiple disappointments and decide to keep fighting? Who could do that? My son can. Who could watch his peers pass by him by--many getting married and some having children of their own--and decide to step back, re-evaluate, and start fresh? Who on earth could do that? My son can. Who could be beaten blow after blow by circumstances and situations and choose to get up, dust off, and fight back? Who could do that? My son can. When others may have wondered if God had forsaken him, turned his back on him, or maybe forgotten him, who could continue to put his faith and trust in God knowing none of that is true?

I will tell you who--MY son can.

In addition to being blessed by Joni, Michael, and Ben, I have also shared in creating lifetime memories with all three of them.

I loved taking an annual trip with just my boys to ride four wheelers at Trace State Park in North Mississippi. We would put on coveralls and go ride along the 20+ miles of muddy ATV trails, come back, shuck our clothes, hose off, cook out, go to sleep, and get up and do it all over again. I loved the time spent taking trips with Ben and Michael individually when they were little to out-of-town karate tournaments. I would take

Ben to Mobile, Meridian, and several other places. We would spend the night, eat out, and have a great time. Michael and I went to a karate tournament in Houston once. We flew together on a big plane and visited the Johnson Space Center while we were there. Michael and I flew to Tampa on one of my business trips, and we went to a pro-hockey game and had backstage passes to a Casting Crowns concert. I took Ben to work one day at the PGA TOUR event and put him on a TV set and let him hold a microphone next to the commentator.

As a family we would go to Branson almost every Christmas and every Fourth of July. Branson is near where my parents retired so we would visit them and then spend four days in Branson. One winter it snowed heavily, so we went to Wal-Mart and bought four inner tube tires, filled them with air at a gas station, and spent the entire day sliding down a hill on a vacant lot. In the summers we would rent a fancy ski boat and wake board and tube on the Table Rock Lake from sunup to sundown. At night we would go to the Dixie Stampede or Kirby Van Burch's magic show. We loved going to what we called the Singing Diner, where all of the waiters and waitresses were also singers, and would take turns singing to the customers. One Easter we all flew to Houston and went to church for Easter services and then took in an Astro's baseball game. We all four took our first international mission trip to earthquake ravaged Haiti. I spent the entire week in awe watching my boys form relationships with Haitian children and display the love of Christ through their words and actions. We built thousands of fantastic and lasting family memories that far outweigh the couple of bumps in the road described in earlier chapters. And believe me, as crazy as some of those things sounded, that is all they were, nothing more than bumps in the road.

I love my family, and I am SO proud of my boys.

If you have read this far, you probably figured out that I am a Christian and I believe the Bible to be true. Do I understand it all? No. Do I believe God created me and has a plan for my life? Yes. Do I believe God created Ben and Michael and has a plan and purpose for their lives? Yes. Did Ben cheat death multiple times? You would expect me to say yes, but my answer is no. Here's why: "Our God is a God who saves; from the Sovereign Lord comes escape from death" (Psalm 68:20, NIV).

Ben's work is not yet done on this earth or he would not still be here.

I firmly believe this. God created him for a purpose. Yes Ben cheated death more than once, but in my opinion it was only by the grace of God that death was cheated. Some of you might wonder if God really saved Ben from death, then why did He allow Ben to be put in danger of death in the first place? Again, I do not know, but I do believe God allowed Ben to experience what he has experienced, and God will somehow use it down the road for His glory. Since I have quoted Scripture, you might expect me to answer with one of the most famous verses of all, "God works in mysterious ways." There is only one problem with that statement. "God works in mysterious ways" is not a verse in the Bible. But there is a verse that comes to a similar conclusion: "And we know that God causes everything to work together for the good of those who love God and are called according to his purpose for them" (Romans 8:28, NLT).

I believe both my boys not only know God, but also love Him. Romans 8:28 emphasizes that God will cause everything to work together for those who love Him; for those who have been called according to his purpose. Has Ben been called according to God's purpose? Yes, we all have, and here are a few verses that explain why I believe that as well as believe He created us for a specific purpose:

> *"For you created my inmost being; you knit me together in my mother's womb."* (Psalm 139:13, NIV)

"O Lord, you have examined my heart and know everything about me." (Psalm 139:1, NLT)

"And even the very hairs on your head are all numbered." (Matthew 10:30, NIV)

"God created man in His own image, in the image of God He created him; male and female He created them." (Genesis 1:27, NASB)

"I knew you before I formed you in your mother's womb. Before you were born I set you apart and appointed you as my prophet to the nations." (Jeremiah 1:5, NLT)

"From one man He has made every nationality to live over the whole earth and has determined their appointed times and the boundaries of where they live." (Acts 17:26, HCSB)

"You saw me before I was born. Every day of my life was recorded in your book. Every moment was laid out before a single day had passed." (Psalm 139:16, NLT)

Plain and simple ladies and gentleman:

YOU are NOT a mistake.

Ben was not a mistake. None of us are a mistake. We were created by God and for God, and none of us are here by accident.

There were times earlier in the book where I referred to certain people in a negative way: Gina as being physically unattractive due to her drug use, Candace as having the sense of a turnip, the worthless piece of garbage head shop owner, and the washed up, has-been former football player now turned foul-mouthed trainer. I said those things because I was angry with each of them, and that is truly how I felt at the time. But hear me clearly; those people are not a mistake either. If God can look at me and see past all the silly things I have done, and look past all of my hate-filled thoughts, and look past all of the sin in my life, and see nothing but a clean slate, He can do the same for them if they have trusted and accepted Jesus into their lives.

We left off in the last chapter with Ben on his way to Treatment Center #4. He completed 42 days of primary treatment and came out with a different attitude than he had when coming out of previous treatments. He was defeated in a way I had never seen before. He celebrated his 23rd birthday on his first full day out of treatment. He moved into a sober living house in Madison. Maybe you remember it as the house from the first chapter: 529 Hunters Creek Circle. His peers already had walked across platforms at universities all across the United States, and had been handed a diploma for their four or more years of studies. While Ben felt like he had squandered several years of his life, he did have some hope. His former boss kept his promise and his job was waiting for him at the Ford dealership. But was that what he truly wanted to do for the rest of his life? He did not know. Did he feel a spiritual connection to God right then? Not really. Could he see himself submitting to an AA sponsor and attending meetings the rest of his life? He knew he needed to, but did not really see himself committing.

He worked hard and got a few dollars in his pocket, then decided it was OK to drop by a casino again. I have heard that the definition of insanity is doing the same thing over and over but expecting a different result. Yes, addiction is a disease, and insanity is a symptom. He won $15,000 at the casino. Sitting in his room one night counting the cash, he thought about how easy it was to win that money. Then he figured if it was that easy to win $15,000, it would be just as easy to turn it into $30,000. He went back to the casino and lost it all, and then he cleaned out his bank accounts, maxed out his credit card, and lost all of that also.

Within a matter of days, he was sticking a needle in his arm in the back yard of 529 Hunters Creek Circle.

Ben was led off in handcuffs that night, and placed in the back of the patrol car.

He was transported to the Madison Police Department for booking, fingerprinting, and processing. Like many city municipalities, the City of Madison does not own or operate a jail. The Sheriff's Department of Madison County owns and operates the county jail, and all of the cities and departments within the county take their prisoners to that facility. So after processing with the city, Ben was transported to the Madison County Jail. The Booking/Detention Officer that night was Michael, his younger brother, who normally would have to process him, take pictures of him, and place him in a cell. Since Ben and Michael were brothers, a supervisor was brought in to oversee the processing. The drugs Ben had taken had worn off somewhat when he arrived at the jail, and Michael had to tell him all he had done because he could not remember any of it.

As I stood in the backyard that night of 529 Hunter's Creek Circle, surrounded by policemen, I felt like there was just no reason for either of us to fight any longer. Ben had fought some good battles, but lost more than he won. Joni and I had fought alongside him and had been injured over and over again. I was tired, and he was tired, and as he was led away in handcuffs I thought maybe it was time to throw in the towel.

We all get to that point occasionally.

But Sam and Kim Kelly would be the first ones to look you in the eye and say suck it up, put *Pride Aside,* and get back in the fight.

A couple of years ago when Ben was sitting in the psych ward before being involuntarily committed to Treatment Center #2, we decided to put legs to the words *Pride Aside* that Joni had texted to friends while Ben lay in the ICU in Oxford. We met with our 18 or so fellow Life Group members from Broadmoor Baptist Church on the morning of October 30, 2011. We decided to share with them publicly for the first time the pain our family was experiencing. They all knew Ben was supposed to be playing football three falls in a row but had never taken the field. Politely they had never asked us why. That morning we spent a few minutes sharing everything we had been through over the last few years, and specifically the last few weeks and days. We then told them we needed their friendship, support, and prayer far more than we needed to maintain our pride. The group stood around us and prayed for us as we sat in our chairs. As I was wiping the tears away from my eyes, I looked down at Joni's black boots, where tears were streaming and splashing on the now wet leather. I glanced up and realized they were not Joni's tears; they were Kim Kelly's tears. Kim and her husband Sam had knelt beside Joni, and Kim was weeping.

Sam and Kim Kelly have known our family for many years. When Ben was in the fifth grade, he had a crush on a cute little girl named Maggie Kate Kelly, the oldest of the Kelly children. Sam Clayton was the middle boy, and Anna Claire was the youngest sister. What none of us realized as the group prayed over Joni and me that morning, while Sam and Kim knelt at Joni's side, was that their son, Sam Clayton, was dying in a car wreck at that exact moment. Sam Clayton Kelly, Walker Kelly, and Mason Wilbanks got up early that beautiful Sunday morning in Madison so they could drive back to Oxford and meet their fraternity's pledge class at church. Our world was in turmoil because our son was navigating a few bumps in the road, but those three families' lives were about to be rocked forever.

Fast-forward to about two and a half years later.

Several people from our Life Group got back together to pray again for the bumps in the road Ben has continued to face. Sam Kelly looked at Joni and me that day and said, "Don't stop fighting. As long as he is breathing, don't stop fighting." Many people have told us that, but nobody has told us that from the perspective of a parent who no longer has the opportunity to fight for his son. What a dishonor it would be to those three families if either Joni or I gave up and stopped fighting now.

Today Ben is at Teen Challenge of the Dakotas in Brookings, South Dakota. Teen Challenge provides care for people of all ages, not just teens, but was originally founded in 1958 as a teen center in Brooklyn, New York. Teen Challenge is not a rehab, per se, although it is designed to provide men and women with an effective and comprehensive Christian faith-based solution to life-controlling drug and alcohol problems. The program in Brookings is 16-months filled with searching the Scriptures and helping people understand God's will for their lives. Ben is allowed two 15-minute phone calls per week, and I am hoping one of those will be today, on Father's Day 2014.

It took a lot of courage for Ben to realize he needed to slow down, back up, quit trying to put a Band-Aid on a gaping wound, focus on himself through long-term treatment, and just start over. It takes a real man to be able to make that type of manly decision. Ben had to get over his many disappointments and dig deep to find a fresh attitude. He had to get over the pain he had suffered and stand up straight and continue to march forward. He had to heal from his bruises and find the strength to fight another day. He had to stop questioning "why me" and decide to seek God first.

Like all of us, Ben also had to put *Pride Aside.*

Afterword

If you would like to stay in touch with Joni and me, to continue to see how God is working through this long journey we have been on, please go to our website, www.prideaside.org. At the site you can:

- Find information on discounted bulk copies of *Pride Aside* to introduce or gift to your church, school, or community.

- Find information on bringing Steve and/or Joni to your church, school, or community to speak to parents and teens about our journey.

- Find additional resources for your church or school such as sermon series notes, bible studies, and other resources.

- Have an opportunity to share your story with us.

- Have an opportunity to follow us on social media.

- Find updates on what has transpired since the book was written. (Samples are included in the next few pages)

Here are ways you can specifically help us continue to support and uplift other families around the country:

- Consider introducing or gifting this book to your church staff. The first person who ever read this book from cover to cover was our pastor, Dr. Rob Futral of Broadmoor Baptist in Madison, Mississippi. He finished the book on a Saturday night and I received the following text from him: *"Just finished your book and don't really have words. Raw, brutally transparent, real, heart-wrenching, inspiring, relatable, frustrating, unsettling, reassuring. A gift of unsettled but secure promise to those who are struggling along the beautiful path of this broken road called life. Thanks for sharing. Praying for that happy ending."* The following Sunday morning he left his seat during our church service and walked over to Joni and me and began to cry. He said, "As a pastor, you don't know how important that was for me to read. I 'knew' everything that was going on, but I didn't 'know.'" By gifting this book to your entire church staff they might get an inside look of what families in your church might be dealing with.

- Consider introducing or gifting this book to your entire church. Many churches give the men a book on Father's Day or the women a book on Mother's Day, and this might make a great gift. Your youth pastor might wish to give this book to all middle school and high school students. Your young adult or median adult pastor may wish to give this book to all of the parents or grandparents in the church.

- Consider introducing or gifting this book to the administrators of your school or possibly to your entire school. I tried to write this book in such a way that both parents and students who read it might get something from it. Parents may be able to pick up on warning signs better, or they may look at some of the things Joni and I did as parents and learn from both our mistakes and successes. One of my biggest prayers, however, is that a student might read this book and it become his or her "Len Bias moment." Maybe something in this book would resonate so powerfully with them that they, like me, would decide never to journey down that dangerous and sometimes fatal path.

- Consider bringing Steve and/or Joni to your church or school to preach in Sunday morning services and/or to speak with parents or teens. If our story could serve as a warning for parents or teens before trouble ever arises, or if it can serve as an encouragement to those who already have experienced heartbreak, then we would be honored to share.

- Like us on Facebook
- Follow us on Twitter

We have decided to keep a running blog of different aspects of our life. We are doing this in hopes that others might be encouraged when God allows a victory to be won, and hopefully pray for us when challenges continue to loom. Many of you who have read this book are facing challenges of your own. While I fully realize you would never wish another family to go through the horror you are personally battling, maybe this book will at least help you realize that you are not alone. There are hundreds of thousands (if not millions) of families around the world who feel the same pain you feel, who are confused by the same things you are confused by, and who are tired and weary just like you are. Just like you, others are seeking clarity instead of confusion, joy instead of despair, assurance instead of self-doubt, and hope instead of hopelessness. You are not alone.

Also, please share your story with us at www.prideaside.org. Do this for two reasons. First, typing or writing and sharing your story will help you. It helped me. It was like I lifted a weight off of my shoulders and it now resides on these pages. Second, we would like to pray for you. I assure you; your story will be prayed over by Joni, me, and many others in our church and community who believe there is incredible power in prayer.

Thank you again, for reading *Pride Aside.*

Below are our first few blog updates found at www.prideaside.org. Join us there for continued updates.

Wednesday, June 18, 2014

Ben called tonight while we were having dinner at a local restaurant. Joni and I left our food sitting on the table and stepped outside to speak to him. I had mentioned in my last letter to him that I went ahead and wrote the book and he was asking me about it. I shared just a few highlights, and he interrupted and brought up the point I had made to him a couple of months ago about the happy ending. He began to cry and said, "I think the happy ending is happening." He shared that he truly feels God has him at the right place at the right time at Teen Challenge in Brookings, SD. His biggest struggle since he has arrived is that he still has horrible compulsive thoughts, OCD type thoughts that consume him for hours at a time. They literally paralyze him, and have for years.

There is one older student there in Brookings that for some reason Ben felt like he wanted to talk to about what was going on in his head. Ben approached him and asked if they could talk. The man said yes, but their schedules are so filled from sun up to sun down, that it would be hard to find the time. After a day had passed, Ben said he was sitting alone and in his mind had decided he no longer was going to share what was going on in his head with this man. As soon as Ben came to that conclusion, the man walked up and said, "Ben, I know we have not found time to get together to talk, but God already told me what you wanted to talk about. God told me last night that you have horrible thoughts in your head, and it is driving you insane. You need to know, I had those thoughts also. Pretty much everyone in here has. They will go away. It took three or four months but my thoughts are now much less frequent. God will take those thoughts away."

Ben talked about these thoughts with his counselor, and his counselor took him to the chapel and said, "You have to cry out to God." Ben literally screamed out, prayed, cried out, yelled, and felt relief coming over his mind and body.

So Joni and I have learned to say this…Today, Ben is good. There was a happy ending to today. Ben is realizing he can cope with the physical and mental challenges he will face as a result of several years of drug abuse and addiction, one day at a time. It is so easy to say, and so hard to do. We both are so proud that he is willing to wake up and fight this disease daily. The disease still lingers, but Ben is still willing to fight it. Your continued prayers for Ben, Michael, and our entire family are still greatly appreciated.

Monday, July 14, 2014

We continue to receive two phone calls a week from Ben, sharply timed at 15 minutes each. He still is very happy to be at Teen Challenge in Brookings, SD. He truly feels like he is beginning to understand what it means to be fully yielded to God, and truly have a relationship with Jesus Christ. Since crying out to God a month ago in the chapel, he no longer has had any drug cravings, or desires to use. Now this is often easy while in treatment (although Teen Challenge is not really treatment, it really is more like a 16-month seminary for those who have struggled in the past). But today, Ben is good. He now has an entirely different set of problems that he wrestles with daily that are not drug related. He now struggles with the guilt of what he has done, the money it has cost, and the relationships he has lost. Joni and I know God will heal those thoughts as well, as long as Ben continues to place his faith and trust in Him. God has already forgiven him, and so have Joni and I, so hopefully soon Ben will be able to forgive himself.

Physically he feels fantastic. He says he loves the food there. He now weighs 167 pounds, which is the most he has ever weighed, which also would have been GREAT during football! They have a fantastic weight room at Teen Challenge of the Dakotas, and he is again benching 300 lbs. That makes him feel so good about himself, and for that we are grateful. TCD has a Facebook page, and I saw a picture of the residents from Sunday singing at a church in Minnesota. Ben looked sharp in his purple dress shirt and silver tie. It was really good to see him.

We have a flight scheduled next week for Joni to be able to go visit Ben. She will leave here next Friday and then the two of them will be able to leave Teen Challenge for eight hours on Saturday. On Sunday Joni will be allowed to attend church with the 32 residents, and then be allowed to spend the afternoon with Ben back at the residence before returning home Monday. She misses her boy. I do too. Joni and I decided to travel there to see Ben separately so he can receive twice the number of visits for the same amount of money. Every other month we are hoping finances will allow one of us to be able to visit him.

Friday, July 25, 2014

I dropped Joni off at the airport this morning, tracked her flight from Jackson, MS to Atlanta, and am now tracking her flight from Atlanta to Minneapolis. There, she will rent a car and make the three-hour drive to Brookings, SD. It has been just over two months since Joni and I dropped Ben off at Teen Challenge of the Dakotas in Brookings. Getting there was a three-day process. We first flew to my parent's house in Northwest Arkansas so he could visit them before beginning his 16-month journey. Our flight was cancelled, so we rented a car and drove from there to South Dakota.

Ben was very quiet over those three days. His spirit was defeated. He kept saying he was looking forward to it, simply because it was something different. He knew he needed something different, but he couldn't identify it. Joni and I knew he needed to fall in love with Jesus, but Ben needed to find this out for himself. And from our twice a week phone calls, we have begun to hear a new Ben emerge.

He called last night, and we updated him on Joni's travel plans. She will arrive in Brookings tonight, and tomorrow she will be allowed to spend eight hours with him off campus, attend church with him Sunday, and then spend another five hours off campus. In order to be granted these privileges, Ben had to 'phase up' from Phase I to Phase II in the Teen Challenge program, which he did earlier this week. In a small ceremony, Ben shared his story with the other men, and shared with them how he now understood how Satan had lied to him for so long, and talked about surrendering his life to Jesus. We asked Ben to share some of the testimony with us, and he said he could not right now without crying. We all know that God has forgiven Ben, but now he has to learn how to forgive himself.

After Joni went to bed last night, I came out to my office to write Ben a letter for Joni to deliver to him.

> *Ben,*
>
> *I wish you somehow could know and feel how proud I am of you. I know you can't imagine that being true, but it is. God has long since forgiven you, the old has passed away, the new has come. My prayer for you is that you forgive yourself. There are two types of guilt found in the Bible. Conviction and Condemnation. Conviction comes from the Holy Spirit, and is good. You felt convicted, and you turned back to God. 1 John 1:9 says "if we confess our sins, He is faithful and just to forgive us*

our sins, and to cleanse us from ALL unrighteousness." You did,
HE did, and it is over, it is in the past. Condemnation comes
from Satan and is meant to tear you down. But Romans 8:1 tells
us it is O.K. "There is therefore now no condemnation for those
who are in Christ Jesus." You can't complete your assignment here
on earth if you allow Satan to mock you and lie to you.

Every time you feel guilt, every time you feel shame, or every
time you feel despair about your past, I want you to laugh out
loud and say, "Satan, you are such an idiot if you think you can
keep that stronghold on me. My God forgave me." God has
an assignment for you to complete. If He didn't, you would not
be here. It may be big, or it may be small, but if you just stay
focused on Him, you will find it and you will complete it.

I miss you so much. I want to call or text you every day. But
I am so happy you are spending this time learning who you are
in Christ. I promise, it is so cool when you find your assignment,
and then realize how God has been preparing you for that
assignment all along and you didn't even know it.

> *Put Pride Aside,*
> *Dad*
> *Prov 16:18*

Thursday, August 14, 2014

I love sitting on the front row. Don't you? Think about it. When
you brag to your friends about the tickets you got to the basketball game,
you brag even louder when they are courtside, front row. Concert tickets,
wouldn't you love to be on the front row? A friend of ours got us tickets
to a Texas Rangers baseball game when Ben was about nine and Michael
was about six; Box #1, Row #1, Seats #1, #2, #3, and #4. Front row!

We could high-five the guy in the batter's box by the third base dugout. We were not seated behind the dugout; we were seated BESIDE the dugout! Front row. Bob Uecker, Mr. Baseball, once did a commercial and after being booted from his seat at a baseball game announced to the neighboring fans that "I must be on the Front Rooowwwww". At church, Joni and I sit on the front row. You can't beat the legroom when there are no seats in front of you. When we moved back to Madison in 1992 we visited what was to become our home church, and on our first visit there we sat on the front row. You could tell a couple of staff members were confused. They looked at us from across the room and knew they didn't recognize us and thought we might be visitors, but were hesitant to introduce themselves because they also thought we must be regular attendees if we were brave enough to sit on the front row.

Today I humbly sat on the 15th row at Broadmoor Baptist Church. Today I didn't want to be on the front row, although there were many times over the last several years in which I thought I might be thrust onto the front row in this setting. The front row today was reserved for the family of Parker Rodenbaugh as the community gathered to celebrate Parker's life. Parker's father, Rick, held tightly to the arm of his lovely wife Cordie, as she struggled on wobbly legs to make her way to the front row. Parker, a 22-year-old student at Mississippi State University and a graduate of Madison Central High School, died early Sunday morning of a drug overdose, shortly after making his way back to the MSU campus for the fall semester.

Many of Parker's friends paid a teary tribute to him from the platform. They described him as handsome, a young man with a perfect smile and brilliant eyes, a friend who knew when to make you laugh and comforted you when you cried. I was so thankful today that I was not seated on the front row, and so saddened as I watched those who were. You would think as much as Joni and I had prepared ourselves over the years for such a day that if anyone in the room could understand how those on the front row felt today, it would be us. Yet, I have no idea what they are experiencing. Not even close. As much pain as we have felt navigating our bumps in the road, I am reminded once again today, for our family they have only been bumps in the road. I thank God again for giving us every day He has given us with Ben and Michael, and pray for the Rodenbaughs and other families we know personally who no longer can see the perfect smile or brilliant eyes of their son or daughter.

Steve and Ben 1992

Ben's toy lawnmower from Chapter 7

Steve and Ben 1993

Steve, Ben and Michael 1994

Christmas card photo 1994

Christmas card photo 1997

Branson vacation 1997

Steve, Ben and Michael 1999

2004 baseball photo mentioned in Chapter 2

Christmas card photo / Disney vacation 2004

Branson vacation 2007

Ben with Steve's parents (Ben and Sue) 2008

One of our favorite photos of a little fan trying to get Ben's attention

Ben leading his teammates onto the field 2008

Ben's record setting game against St. Andrews 2008

Christmas card photo 2008

Ben with Coach Larry Fedora at University of Southern Mississippi 2009

Media Day at University of Southern Mississippi 2009

Ben with Coach Houston Nutt at the University of Mississippi 2009

Christmas card 2011 mentioned in Chapter 17

Steve, Joni, Michael, and Ben in Haiti 2012

Ben and his two friends (JonVeel and Bajou) in Haiti 2012

Ben in Haiti 2012

Michael, Carrol (Joni's dad), and Ben
before leaving for Teen Challenge in 2014